If We Make It 'til Daylight

The Story of Frank Mays

and the Sinking of the *Carl D. Bradley*

as told to

Pat & Jim Stayer

and Tim Juhl

The *Carl D. Bradley* -- Lost on Lake Michigan
November 18th, 1958
Photo Credit-Paula Rollins

Additional copies may be purchased from:
Out of the Blue Productions
4658 S. Lakeshore
Lexington, MI 48450
www.outoftheblueproductions.net

Front cover artwork by Bob McGreevy
Back cover photo credit: Robert Fitz

60th Anniversary Printing - 2018

ISBN-978-0-9627084-9-7

Dedication

I wish to dedicate this book to my 33 shipmates who perished in the sinking of the *Carl D. Bradley*. May their families find peace.

I also wish to commend the bravery of the crews of the U.S. Coast Guard Cutters *Sundew* and *Hollyhock*, as well as the Coast Guard Aviators that searched for me throughout that terrible night on Lake Michigan.

No less brave were the crews of the many merchant ships that risked themselves and their vessels to come to our aid.

For those selfless acts and the many kindness I have received throughout the years, I am eternally grateful.

Frank Mays

Acknowledgements

The authors would like to thank the following people for their help in making this book possible:

From the *USCGC Sundew*: The authors are indebted to Captain Harold Muth, Robert Fitz, Warren Toussaint, and John (Jack) Coppens for sharing their stories of incredible valor and heroism of how they fought the seas to rescue the crew of the ill-fated *Carl D. Bradley*.

Bradley explorers: We are grateful to our friends, Bernie Hellstrom and Mirek Standowicz, for sharing their stories.

From Rogers City: The authors would like to thank Jeanette Brege, Frank's friend and neighbor in 1958, for sharing her recollections. In addition, we would like to acknowledge the assistance of the *Great Lakes Lore Museum*.

Artwork: We are extremely grateful to Bob McGreevy for the many hours he put into the painting displayed on this book's front cover. By working with Frank Mays, Bob's picture is the most accurate depiction of the final moments of the *Carl D. Bradley* that has been produced.

Photo archives: The authors greatly appreciate the wealth of photos and knowledge that Ralph Roberts and Fr. Pete Van Der Linden shared with us. We would also like to thank Bob Campbell and Paula Rollins for the use of their photos.

Research: A special thanks to our good friends Cris Kohl, Joan Forsberg, Bob Geno, Steve Moore, and Gareth McNabb for all of the research and knowledge they have shared with us. We would also like to thank Gerald F. Micketti for allowing us to use information from his book, *The Bradley Boats*.

Editors: We would like to thank Wendy Juhl, Joan Juhl, Betty Currie, Cary Stayer, Doloras Muth, Deb Dudeck, Renee Allen, and Gloria Johnston for the countless hours they spent editing this book. Their efforts are greatly appreciated. Special thanks to Kristen (Juhl) Pennock for her graphic design expertise and help preparing this book for printing.

For his inspiration and encouragement: We honor the memory of the late Dennis Hale, sole survivor of the *Daniel J. Morrell*.

Contents

Tuesday Evening, November 18, 1958

It all seems unreal. My name is Frank Mays and just a short time ago I was going about my business as a deckwatch aboard the freighter, *Carl D. Bradley*. Now, I am fighting for my life, clinging to a tiny raft as it falls between mountainous waves on storm-lashed Lake Michigan.

All I can do is lie on the raft and endure. The cold November wind cuts through my wet clothing like a knife.

Three other *Bradley* crewmen share the raft, each just as miserable as I am. Huddling together we try to shelter each

Frank and Elmer Fleming help Gary Strzelecki onto the Raft
© Robert McGreevy

other from the deadly wind--but to no avail. Our hands grow numb as we grip the small slats of wood that make up the deck. Time has lost all meaning. The night is black as coal, and we get little warning before the monster waves hit us. I've never felt so cold and helpless.

What little conversation there was on the raft has pretty much ended, leaving each of us to our own thoughts. I think back to how my day began, a lifetime ago.

The *Carl D. Bradley* leaving port
Photo Credit--ML Screenings

1 *Last Trip of the Season*

"It's 3:30. Good morning!" announced Gary Strzelecki, the 12 to 4 deckwatch, as he stuck his head into our cabin. I shook the sleep from my eyes as his words registered. It was time for me to rise and begin my four to eight watch. Above me, I could hear Gary Price stirring in his bunk. One of the younger fellows on the ship, Price was a deckhand on my watch. Yawning, I stretched for a minute, collected my thoughts, and pulled back the heavy curtains that surrounded my bunk. Looking about in the dim light, I saw my clothes draped over the chair where I had left them after my previous watch. Next to them was my old green navy foul weather jacket with its fur collar and thick lining. I would need it on this cold November morning.

Gary Price
Photo Credit--ML Screenings

1

Gary Price was moving faster than I was; I could see his silhouette as he finished dressing. I dressed quickly and with a brief glance, indicated to him that I was ready to leave. There was no conversation, because we didn't want to wake our roommates, Dennis Meredith and Duane Berg, who were asleep in their bunks. They had worked the 8 to 12 watch and would be back on duty in another four hours. We slipped out of the room as noiselessly as possible and headed to the galley for coffee.

Our cabin was in the forward end of the ship while the galley was in the after section. We quickened our pace as we walked along the open deck in the cold morning air. I pulled the collar of my jacket up and gazed out across the water at the lights on shore. The land was just shadows in the blackness of the night, so the lights made it appear as if we were looking at stars from an unknown galaxy, resting on the water. We must be near Milwaukee, I thought, calculating in my head how far we should have traveled since leaving Gary, Indiana, late the night before. We were on our way to Manitowoc, Wisconsin, where the *Bradley* was scheduled to have a new cargo hold installed. With a little luck, we would be at the dry dock in Manitowoc by later that afternoon. The seas weren't too bad, so we should make good time.

When Gary opened the galley door, we were greeted by the warmth from the ovens and the aroma of brewing coffee. Night cook, Alfred Pilarski, had been hard at work, insuring that none of us would go hungry. I poured myself a cup of black coffee, grabbed a sweet snack, and enjoyed a minute or two of conversation before heading forward to the pilothouse to take coffee up to the crew there. Gary Price remained behind, enjoying the company of the other crewmen, knowing I would return later.

Alfred Pilarski
Photo Credit--ML Screenings

I walked back out on deck and took my normal route down the port side of the ship. I always walked on the port side (left side of the ship as you face the bow), unless there were strong winds and spray coming over the railing. Then I would cross over to the starboard side or take the tunnel below the cargo hold. As I walked forward, I was vaguely aware of the waves slapping against the hull. They were probably six feet high. Such waves could toss a small boat around violently, but they had little effect on the 638-foot *Bradley*.

Arriving at the bow, I climbed up the two decks to the pilothouse. My cabin was on the main deck. On the level above were the chart room, the first and second mate's quarters, and Captain Roland Bryan's room. I imagine Captain Bryan was probably asleep at this time of night. I didn't see him on my watch very often. In the pilothouse, first mate Elmer Fleming would be in command of the *Bradley*.

I hadn't met the captain before I went to sail with him on the *Carl D. Bradley*. However, Roland Bryan had a reputation for being a well-seasoned captain. I had faith in him. After all, he was a captain and I was a deckwatch. He had started

3

sailing at the age of 14 and had over 38 years on the lakes, the last 11 as a captain. For the last four, he had been the master of the *Bradley*.

Captain Roland Bryan
Photo Credit--ML Screenings

Bryan was not the first captain that I had sailed with. I started working for U.S. Steel in the spring of 1957, sailing on the steamer *Rogers City*. I stayed with her all of that year, then helped lay her up in Manitowoc, Wisconsin. The rest of that winter, I worked on the boats that were laid up in Rogers City.

In the spring of 1958, business wasn't too good for U.S. Steel. Orders for steel were down and the decision was made to leave some of the boats in lay-up. With no seniority, that left me without a job. However, one fellow on the steamer *Calcite* hurt himself at home, and I was asked to fill in for him until he could return to work. I sailed on the *Calcite* most of that spring. Then another job opened up on the steamer *Clymer* for a few weeks. After I left the *Clymer*, I sat on shore for a while until a job opened up on the *Cedarville*. I stayed with her until October, when the decision was made to bring the *Carl D. Bradley* out of lay-up.

4

The *Bradley* needed an AB deckwatch. "AB" stands for "able-bodied," a seaman's term. When you start out on the deck, you begin as a seaman. You do some studying, take a test, and then you get your AB papers, which I had. The job on the *Bradley* was a permanent position, so when it was offered to me, I gladly took it. The *Carl D. Bradley* had been the flagship of the Bradley Transportation Company, and had once been known as the "Queen of the Lakes." She was older now and much in need of repair. I was sure that Captain Bryan was looking forward to getting his ship into drydock at the end of the season.

I was in no hurry as I carried the coffee up the two flights of steps to the waiting pilothouse crew. The steel pipes that made up the railings were perfectly spaced for a workingman's

First Mate Elmer Fleming
Photo Credit--Presque Isle County Advance

shoulder span, making a solid hand hold for a man to grab onto during rough weather. The railings were undoubtedly cold today, but my fur lined work gloves protected me.

I climbed the stairs with care, taking a minute to stop on the platform between the flights, and looked out across the dark water. I felt safe and secure on the giant *Bradley* and took a moment to enjoy the peacefulness of the night. I would work most of this watch in the dark, for it was November eighteenth, and the sun would not rise for several hours.

Ray Kowalski
Photo Credit--ML Screenings

When I opened the pilothouse door, Elmer Fleming and Ray Kowalski greeted me with smiles as I handed them their coffee. Coffee was just as important to the running of the ship as the coal was for the boilers. When we had a free hand, there was often a coffee cup in it. I asked Elmer about the *Bradley's* progress, and he told me he anticipated we would be tied up in the Manitowoc shipyard sometime between two and four that afternoon. We shared opinions as to how long it would take to put the *Bradley* into drydock with the consensus being that we should be home for Thanksgiving. I remember talking to Elmer and Ray about being home for the holidays. Rogers City was the homeport for the "Bradley Boats" and most of the crew lived in the area. Rogers City is a small company town, and everyone knew everyone else.

In fact, when I was growing up, Elmer lived across the street from us in an apartment. But I was in high school and much younger than he was.

Talk soon turned to the weather. The winds were blowing 25 to 35 MPH when we left Gary, Indiana, but the forecast was calling for gale force winds of 50 to 65 MPH from the south-southwest. Fortunately, this shouldn't concern us, as we wouldn't be heading out into the open lake.

Elmer had no orders for Gary and I at the moment, so I turned up the collar of my old jacket and headed back to the galley, where I joined Gary and the others gathered there. We drank coffee and talked until about 6:00 AM, when Mel Orr came by and gave Gary and I orders to go down in the tunnel. There was some work there that had to be done.

Mel Orr
Photo Credit--ML Screenings

The "Bradley Boats" were designed to carry stone. Their cargo holds ran from just behind the crew quarters in the bow to just ahead of the coalbunker near the stern. Behind the coal bunker is the engine room. If one looked at the cross section of the cargo hold, they would find it was shaped somewhat

7

like a "W." At the bottom points of the "W" were two large conveyor belts. The belts carried the stone forward from the cargo hold and dumped it into a chute, which funneled it to the bucket elevator. The stone was then brought up to the main deck, where it was transferred to another conveyer belt on the unloading boom. The unloading boom would then be swung out over the side and the stone unloaded. These ships were called self-unloaders as compared to "straight-deckers" which required dockside unloading equipment.

The open space below the cargo hold, between the two conveyer belts, was called the tunnel. The floor of the tunnel was the top of the ballast tanks. A person could walk through the tunnel to go forward or aft without having to go out into the elements. It was dark and dirty, but at least it was out of the weather. After unloading stone at Gary, it was the job of the deck crew to wash the tunnel down.

Finishing my watch at 8:00 AM, I had a large breakfast of eggs and bacon and then headed back to my room. I lay down in my bunk and read a little before taking a long nap.

2 *Change of Plans*

When I awoke later that afternoon, I immediately knew that the company's plans for the *Bradley* had changed. It was evident from the pitching and rolling of the ship that we were no longer in the shelter of the Wisconsin shoreline. Captain Bryan must have received new orders. I threw back my curtain and let my eyes slowly adjust to the daylight. I speculated on what our new plans were as I finished pulling on my heavy, steel-toed work shoes. I'd never find out by sitting in my cabin, so I slipped on my jacket, grabbed my work gloves, and stepped out into the companionway.

It was 3:30 in the afternoon when I headed up to the pilothouse to see Elmer and find out what was going on. While I was napping, the captain had received instructions to return to Rogers City for one more load of stone. When the *Bradley* neared Cana Island, the captain ordered a course change to a heading of 046°, which took us right out into the lake, in the direction of Lansing Shoal. That explained the different motion I had felt in my cabin. Elmer said he had reduced the engine speed by ten RPM because of the rougher conditions, but we were still making about 15 knots. Oh well, I thought as I headed back to the galley for a cup of coffee.

As was my habit, I walked along the port side on my way to the stern. It was much colder than before. Outside the shelter of the Wisconsin shore, the gusting wind sometimes carried spray from the waves onto the deck.

The waves, which were now approaching 20 feet, were causing the *Bradley* to pitch and roll as we pushed further into Lake Michigan. As rough as it was, we probably wouldn't be doing much work today.

The *Carl D. Bradley* in rough seas
Photo Credit--ML Screenings

Arriving back at the galley, I got some coffee and a bite to eat. I then returned to the pilothouse with coffee for the guys there. As I entered, First Mate Elmer Fleming had just finished giving Mel Orr and Gary Price some orders and they were headed down below. Concerned about the watertight integrity of the ship in the rising seas, Elmer told me to go back aft and check the coalbunker. He wanted me to make sure it was secured, pinned and clamped, so that the hatch sections couldn't come lose. Leaving the warmth of the pilothouse, I walked along the deck to the coalbunker and spent a few minutes making sure all was secure.

The *Bradley's* Galley

Photo Credit--ML Screenings

With that job finished, I decided it wouldn't hurt to waste a little time, so I went down into the engine room to visit with the engineers and anyone else that happened to be there. The warmth felt good after the exposed deck. I decided to gradually work my way down to the tunnel and follow it back to the bow. In the engine room, I stopped and spoke with Alfred Boehmer. I knew Alfred from high school, and his wife Dolores had graduated with my brother. We always called her Angie, because her last name was Andrzejewski. She was the sweetest thing. I think she was well liked by everybody in town.

Leaving the engine spaces, I went into the stoker room, where I talked to Paul Heller for a while. Paul lived just down the street from me in Rogers City. He was older than me, but I knew some younger members of his family. When I first

Alfred Boehmer
Photo Credit--ML Screenings

on board, we talked about living in Rogers City and about his family, and we soon became friends. Today, we chatted about the change in sailing orders, when we should be getting in to port, and how it would affect our plans.

After leaving the stoker room, I strolled down to the tunnel. The overhead structure of the tunnel was actually the bottom of the cargo hold, which was empty on this trip. Looking upwards I thought that it was a good thing that these old holds were being replaced. There was rust and holes on the top and sides, even near the bulkhead where the holds were attached to the hull. It was a common joke amongst the *Bradley's* crew that the old girl was held together by rust.

When the deck crew washed off the unloading boom, water would run into the cargo hold and leak down into the tunnel. Water would also spray up from the floor of the tunnel, which you'll remember was actually the top of the ballast tanks, or "tank tops" as we called them. In fact, some of rivets that held the plates on the ballast tanks were leaking or missing, and water would squirt up so high that I could take a board and deflect the water to hit the back of an unsuspecting gate operator on the other side of the tunnel. We used to do that to each other as a prank.

Paul Heller
Photo Credit--ML Screenings

Because the stern of the *Bradley* rode lower in the water than the bow, any water that found its way into the hold would collect near the after end. When I entered the tunnel, I could see two or three feet of water underneath the floor grate, so I took the time to sump it out. As I worked in the tunnel, I heard the *Bradley* creaking and groaning as it twisted and turned through the angry seas. I'd heard such sounds before and thought little about it. Maybe the new cargo hold would help strengthen the old girl.

When I finished in the tunnel, I continued on my way forward until I reached the dunnage room. There, amongst the paint, ladders, lines and shovels, I met Gary Price, who had finished the job Elmer had sent him on earlier. With time to kill, I sat down on a coil of rope and lit up a cigar while Gary pulled out a cigarette. We decided to wait here, out of the weather, knowing that if the mate needed us, he would ring a bell to get our attention. We chatted as sailors do under such circumstances, speculating as to our chances of being off watch when we arrived at Rogers City.

We had just put out our smokes when, all of a sudden, there was this deafening thud. It reverberated through the ship like a sonic boom echoing in a canyon. Immediately, the boat began to shake violently. For an instant we sat startled, knowing something major had happened, but what? Did we hit another ship? Was it an explosion? Without thinking, we jumped to our feet and that was when a second thud, just as ominous as the first, came from somewhere deep below in the tunnel. The dunnage room was nowhere to be in an emergency, so I rushed up the ladder with Gary right behind. Grabbing the railings, we propelled ourselves up the steps so fast that we only hit every other one as we went. The loud ringing of the general alarm bell spurred us on even faster, and it seemed like we climbed the two flights of stairs in a matter of seconds. Reaching the main deck, we threw open the door and raced out to see what had happened.

It was dusk now and the ship's lights were all on. The waves were running high and we had following seas, seas that hit the stern first. In such conditions, a large wave can lift the stern so high that the rudder and propeller come right out of the water.

14

Looking aft, we couldn't see the stern. At first, I thought my eyes hadn't adjusted to the darkness, but as I stared, the stern section slowly rose into view. I immediately knew we were in big trouble, but the gravity of the situation hadn't totally sunk in. Instinctively, I ran to our room, which was probably ten feet away, and Gary followed. We had to close the door to get our lifejackets, because they were on a rack overhead. I took a moment to grab my watch and wallet from my dresser drawer and then stepped back outside. When we came back out, I saw the stern still rising in and out of view with the motion of the waves.

It was quite obvious to me that the keel of the ship had broken and the *Bradley* was doomed. In the back of my mind, I realized that water must be rushing into the tunnel where I had walked just minutes before. We were at the mercy of the lake and really taking a beating. The stern began to move even more violently, flapping up and down, like the whipping of a dog's tail. Just then, the whistle blew seven short blasts and one long. The captain had ordered us to abandon ship.

My life-saving station was in the stern where I was to help launch a lifeboat, but I knew that I could never make it back across the flexing deck. Instead, I crossed from the port side to the starboard, where I could see that we were still like a piece of metal bending very, very severely. "Top side to the life raft I yelled," as I sprinted to the ladder with Gary right behind me.

When we reached the pilothouse deck, Ray Kowalski was still at the wheel, and Elmer Fleming was leaning out the port door of the pilothouse. He did not have a lifejacket on, having apparently given them all out to the men that arrived at the pilothouse without one. He was standing there looking aft; with the cord to the radiophone running over his shoulder back into the pilothouse. My blood ran cold as I heard him shout into the handset, "Mayday! Mayday! This is the *Carl D. Bradley*. We are 12 miles southwest of Gull Island. We are breaking in two and sinking. Any ships in the area, please come to our aid." He repeated the "Mayday" message over and over until we lost power and the radio died.

No one seemed to know what to do next. The captain was standing behind the pilothouse surrounded by a crowd of men. Most of the guys that worked in the forward end were there. I recall seeing Mel Orr, Joseph Krawczak, Dick Book, Duane Berg, Paul Greengtski and Earl Tulgetske in this group. I didn't see conveyormen Edward Vallee or Leo Promo, Jr., or third mate Carl Bartell.

The captain was busy talking to the second mate, John Fogelsonger. The other guys were just milling around. At this point, Gary and I separated, and that was the last time I saw him. As he joined the crowd by the captain, I went across the deck to the port side, where my second cousin, Alva Budnick, was standing. Then Elmer said, "Someone get the life raft ready." No one else was moving, so I did. The life raft sat on its own section of decking behind the pilothouse. It rested on a cradle, with the theory being that, when the water reached that level, the raft would simply float off. I wasn't sure it would work that easily, for it seemed to be glued in place by the layers of orange paint it had received over the years. I jumped on the raft, dropped to my knees, and began to untie the raft and the oars that were stored with it. As my hands worked feverishly at the bindings, my eyes were drawn to the spectacle of the giant *Bradley* tearing herself apart.

John Fogelsonger
Photo Credit--ML Screenings

Under the lights on the main deck, I could see John Fogelsonger running toward the stern. I assumed he was heading off to do whatever it was he and the captain had been talking about. Then, as if it were paper, the huge steel plates of the deck began to tear apart somewhere near the tenth hatch on the port side. With sparks flying, the tear quickly ripped across the deck. As the gash began to grow, I saw John run toward the crack and leap into the air. I didn't see him land. He just disappeared between the two parts of the ship. The bow and stern continued to separate at an amazing rate, with cables snapping, and blue and red flashes illuminating the darkening sky. Suddenly the lights on the forward end of the ship went dark, and the general alarm went silent, as the cables bringing power to the bow were severed.

As the rip in the deck widened, the bow started to pivot to the left. The stern and the bow were no longer in a straight line. That brought the seas against our starboard side, while the stern continued forward, driven by the waves crashing against the stern. With the waves hitting us broadside now, the bow began to pitch and roll from starboard to port.

With nothing more he could do, Ray abandoned the wheel and exited the pilothouse on the starboard side. Elmer dropped the useless phone and ran below to his cabin to grab a lifejacket, a task made difficult by the total darkness. He returned in less than two minutes and reported that the main deck was awash. That meant the main deck was now underwater. We were sinking.

The bow of the *Bradley* began to list to the port. Out of the corner of my eye, I saw the captain move to the high side of the ship, followed by most of the men. I remained on the raft, still on my knees, waiting.

Suddenly, a massive wave struck. The *Bradley's* bow pitched violently to the port side, catapulting the raft and me about 20 feet through the air. It hit the water almost vertically on one of its pontoons, but I, amazingly, stayed with it. My relief was short-lived, because as the raft bounced and then tipped in the water, I was hurled off with such force that I was driven deep below the water's surface. I was stunned for a moment as the bubbles rushed passed my face. Recovering quickly, with several quick strokes and the buoyancy of my lifejacket, I was at the surface in no time. Gasping for air, I cleared the water from my eyes and looked around, seeing nothing. Not knowing of anything better to do, I put my head down and took my first stroke. As I brought my arm around and down, my forearm slammed against the raft. It must have been blown toward me or slid back down a wave. Either way, I was relieved to see it.

18

I grabbed the raft and started to climb aboard. By working my foot onto a small ledge that ran lengthwise along the nearest pontoon and holding onto the guide rail, I was able to scramble onto the platform and get out of the water within a minute.

Looking around me, I saw a man reaching for the raft. As he started to climb up, I grabbed the shoulders of his lifejacket and pulled. He looked up and I saw it was Elmer Fleming. With my help, he struggled up on to the raft. Together, we scanned the water for others and started yelling, "We're over here. We have the raft." We knew the only way we could rescue anybody would be for them to come to us. The oars were gone and we had no way to propel the raft. Trying to paddle a raft in those seas would have been a waste of effort. I don't know if anyone ever heard us over the roar of the wind and waves, but we kept shouting.

Gary Strzelecki
Photo Credit--ML Screenings

Within minutes, we spotted Gary Strzelecki. He swam strongly over to us and started to climb up. Elmer and I quickly grabbed his arms and pulled him aboard. All this

19

time, we were still yelling and scanning the water for others. Then we spotted Dennis Meredith as the raft drifted toward him. We all worked quickly to get him on board.

Dennis Meredith
Photo Credit--ML Screenings

In the darkness, we could hear men yelling but we couldn't see anybody. Gary insisted that he should leave the raft and try to find his brother-in-law, Ray Kowalski. Elmer tried to talk him out of it. He declared, "You can't go. Stay aboard! We can't see him." Gary kept pleading, "I want to get to him. I want to help him. I got to find him."

Elmer insisted, "You can't find him. You can't see over these waves, and you will never find your way back to the raft. We don't know where he is now." The last time I saw Ray, he had come out of the pilothouse and was on the deck. We had no way of knowing where he ended up when he was thrown into the water. The waves were so high that he could have drifted away or be in the trough of the next wave, and we would never see him. Reluctantly, Gary stayed aboard. Even as the waves broke over him, he never took his eyes off the water, hoping to see Ray.

Soon, all we could hear was the wind whistling and the waves crashing around us. Unwilling to give up hope, we continued to yell. Though it was just dusk when the ship started to sink, it was now dark. The wind-driven spray made it almost impossible to see.

Looking in the distance, we could barely make out a man with his arms stretched high over his head. As I yelled to him, I could tell it was Mel Orr. We watched Mel rise to the crest of the wave and then disappear as he rolled down the backside. As we rose to the top of the next wave, we anxiously searched for him, but we saw nothing. We saw no crew, no wreckage, and no debris around us. The forward section of the ship was just gone. We continued to scan the waves, but we never saw another person after that.

Thinking it over later on, I believe I know why so few men made their way to the raft. When the bow was listing, most of the guys followed the captain up to the high side. The wave that hit us and knocked the raft loose made the bow roll so violently that I think the guys with the captain were catapulted quite a distance away. If I had been with them instead of on the raft, I probably wouldn't have made it either.

3 *Alone*

The bow of the *Bradley* was gone, but amazingly the stern was still there. It was floating on an even keel, ablaze with lights. Except for the missing bow section, she looked as if nothing had happened. From our vantage point on the raft, we could see the after cabins clearly. I saw the lifeboat, hanging unattended from its davits. It had been swung out over the water, which could only be done using a manual crank. Someone had attempted to prepare the lifeboat for launch, but where was the crew? We never saw anybody.

After what seemed like a minute or two, the stern section suddenly began to pivot, wheel (propeller) up. We watched with amazement as the massive propeller came totally out of the water. The stern continued to rise, gaining speed as she went. All of a sudden, the momentum seemed to stop, as the aft-section towered above the waves with all her lights aglow. Then she began to plunge straight down. As the white of the after cabins reached water level, there was a tremendous blast. Her hot, steam-filled boilers had exploded as they contacted the icy lake water. The stern was briefly engulfed in red flames and black smoke before it was extinguished by her dive to the bottom, some 380 feet below.

No one on the raft said a word--everybody just stared over the water to where the ship had been. With the lights of the stern gone, the darkness was total. There was no moon, and the dense cloud cover obscured the stars. We felt alone and totally isolated. Now it was only the four of us.

The *Bradley's* final plunge
© Robert McGreevy

At this point, we were all alert. I remember Elmer telling us about a ship that was nearby, the German motor vessel, *Christian Sartori*. He was sure that she had heard our "Mayday" message. He knew she was monitoring channel 51 and would certainly be on her way. He cautioned us that it would be a while before she got here, "But we'll be alright," he said, which encouraged everybody. There was a lot of discussion then.

Elmer took charge. He was the senior officer and was the most experienced of all of us. He pried open the center storage compartment of the raft where there were three flares and a sea anchor. Elmer took out one of the flares, pulled off the cap and struck it. Instantly, a red flame ignited just inches above his hands. He held the flare high over his head, looking like a kid with a large Fourth of July sparkler, except it was a glaring red. The flare's bright flame kindled a spirit of hope in our hearts. It illuminated our raft, and we all watched intently until its flame died.

Hoping for rescue, we all scanned the horizon looking for a ship, but the inky blackness combined with violent waves pitched and rolled us so much that it was hard to keep our orientation. Even so, our spirits were high, and we talked amongst ourselves. About a half an hour later, Elmer struck the second flare and it, too, burst into brilliant light. The flare's sizzling sound was barely audible against the wailing wind and the deafening crash of waves, and yet, that didn't really seem to bother us at this point.

Elmer tucked the other flare deep inside his jacket to keep it dry. He encouraged all of us to hold on, certain that help was coming. He said someone had surely heard our "Mayday" and help was on the way. We clung to the raft and talked about our forthcoming rescue. Soon, the lights of a ship, possibly the *Christian Sartori*, appeared in the distance. She was coming toward us. A sense of warmth filled us, as relief replaced our fear. Conversation ended, as each man was left with his own thoughts. I remember thinking, "Oh boy! We're going to get on board, get dry and have something to eat and drink. We're going to be all right!" With renewed energy, we held on and waited. Each time we rose up on the crest of a wave, we could see her lights--then they would disappear as we sank back into the trough.

The *Christian Sartori* was getting closer. We could see her mast light and running lights clearly now, red on the left and green on the right. We knew she was coming directly at us.

To draw the *Sartori's* crew's attention, Elmer pulled out the last flare and struck it, but the flare would not ignite. He struck it again and again like one would strike a wooden match

24

MV Christian Sartori
Photo Credit--Ralph Roberts

against its box, but to no avail. In desperation, he continued
to strike the flare, but with no success. It must have gotten
too wet.

Would the *Sartori* be able to see us in the darkness?
We watched her approach until suddenly, her red light
disappeared, and we saw more of her green light. She was
turning away from us! We knew they hadn't seen us. We were
too far away, and her searchlights could only penetrate a short
distance through the heavy spray. They definitely could not
hear us because of the noise of the sea and the wind. And that
was it... We knew that we were out there for a long ride and
would have to endure whatever Lake Michigan threw at us.

4 *And Then There Were Three...*

The waves continued to build. We crammed our fingers into the 1/2-inch spaces between the boards and held on. Our drenched clothing began to freeze as the relentless waves sprayed us like a sprinkler on a timer. Unlike children who welcome the water on a hot summer day, we cursed each drop. The well-being we felt earlier as the *Christian Sartori* approached had disappeared with her. Elmer and I tried to encourage the others. He said if the *Christian Sartori* was looking for us, so was the Coast Guard. After thinking about that for a while, I added, "If we make it 'til daylight, we will be found."

As I clung to the raft in the darkness, I estimated the waves had grown to 30 feet with the occasional rogue 40 footer. I remember the fear I felt when we were hit by a particularly big one. I knew it was larger by the speed at which the wave sucked the raft up toward its towering crest, then without warning, it tipped us right over. We came crashing down into the trough of the wave. Not prepared for the rafts sudden upheaval, we were stunned as we hit the bone-chilling water. Amazingly, the raft was right alongside when we surfaced.

It took all the strength we had left to crawl back onto the raft. The first man that managed to get aboard, as exhausted as he was, unselfishly assisted the others. Working as a team, we labored until all were back safe on the raft. Once the four of us were back aboard, we huddled as close to each other as we could, trying to generate some warmth. We lay pressed together for a long time, but there was no escaping the cold.

26

If we tried to straighten up, we would be gripped by painful cramps that seemed to take control of our muscles. There was nothing else we could do, so shivering uncontrollably, we waited.

Life rafts of the period were designed with the top and bottom identical, so no matter how it landed, it would always be upright. That part of their design worked well, but the guide rails did not. There were no handles to grab, so if a man let go of the deck, he would easily be washed away. I had little choice but to lay with my chest flat against the boards, my arms bent and my fingers jammed into the spaces between slats. I lay on one hip, my body slightly twisted, my knees as close to my chest as possible.

It took too much energy to look around, so I seldom knew when the next big wave was going to hit. Sometimes Gary would call out, "Hang on, here comes a big one," Otherwise the first warning was when I felt the raft being dragged upward to a near vertical position. For a brief second, the raft would hesitate at the wave's crest, before either sliding down the backside or flipping again and tossing us back in the water. The second time I got dunked, I remember surfacing so close to the raft that I was able to reach it with a single stroke. Even so, I was gasping for breath from the shock of the immersion. I clung to the lifeline strung along the barrel side of the raft, and rested for a moment. The water felt different, and I realized it was now warmer than the air. I wanted to remain in the water, but common sense told me I couldn't. Water will take away body heat more quickly than air. I had to get back on the raft, or I would die here.

The third time the raft flipped over, only three of us made it back on. Dennis Meredith just didn't have the strength. The general alarm probably caught him taking a nap in our room, and he was dressed in only a heavy white sweatshirt, lightweight pants and socks without shoes. The rest of us had been on duty and were wearing jackets that gave us some protection against the cold. Dennis's clothes remained wet and were partially frozen, which significantly lowered his body temperature. This time, Dennis didn't even attempt to climb on the raft. He just hung there without talking. Elmer, Gary and I tried with all the strength we could muster to get him back onto the raft, but we just couldn't do it. I wonder now if maybe his lifejacket was snagged on the raft, holding him back. I just know we couldn't budge him. All this time, Dennis never looked at us or said a word.

We couldn't get Dennis aboard the raft, but there was no way we were going to let him go. Fighting muscle cramps and hypothermia, we grimly held on. Gary took one of Dennis's arms and held it tight between his legs, and I took the other and did the same. I don't know how many hours we held onto him this way, as the passing of time was meaningless to us. Every so often, I would check on Dennis, hoping he could hold on until we were rescued. One time I looked back, and Dennis's head was face down in the water. I reached over and raised his head. His eyes were totally white. There was nothing we could do for him now. He had passed on. I looked at Gary, and without speaking, we simultaneously let his arms slide out from our grasps. Instantly, he was gone. I felt a deep emptiness as I looked where he had been, but there was no sign of him. There was no conversation now, just the cold, the wind, and the waves.

5 *The Sea Anchor Brings Hope*

Sometime later, Elmer got the sea anchor out from the raft's storage compartment. It was cone-shaped, with a diameter of about 13 inches at the mouth, tapering to about six inches at the small end. Made of gray canvas, it measured about three feet overall. I secured it at the center on the back of the raft with a bowline knot, then tossed it overboard. With the sea anchor dragging behind us, we rode smoothly over the smaller waves. When we came to one of the towering monsters that had flipped us before, the raft trembled, but we did not tip. This small success renewed my hope and once more I found myself thinking "If we make it 'til daylight, we will be found."

I lay back down on the raft, relieved to know the raft was more stable and that I wasn't likely to have to struggle to get out of the water again. This brought me a little comfort, though I still had to face the spray from the waves and the gale force wind that pummeled my body.

Lying there my thoughts started to drift. I thought of Dennis and of his older brother George. I had gone to school with both of them, Dennis graduating the year after I did. I pictured his sister, Sandy, who had an apartment on the same floor as mine in the Bruski Building. In my heart, I cried as I pictured her face as she heard about her brother.

I thought about my wife and our three sons. Michael was four now, and he enjoyed the role of older brother. Mark had just turned two. I remember how they reacted when their baby brother, Frank, was born just a month ago. Frank was

Alva Budnick
Photo Credit--ML Screenings

so small in their arms. They were all so young, too young to be without a father. For their sake I decided I must hold on.

In my mind, the face of my cousin Alva appeared. We had been very close, hanging out together all the time. He lived just down the block from me. It was hard to believe that he was gone, along with so many others. A sudden chill ran up my spine, it had just hit me--most of this crew came from Rogers City. The town would be in a total upheaval tonight. Elmer felt that the *Christian Sartori* and the Coast Guard got our "Mayday" message, so others would soon know as well. The news that the *Bradley* had gone down would spread like wildfire. I wondered what the people were going to think when they found out. The *Carl D. Bradley* lost, unthinkable! Never in the company's history had they lost a ship. They had an incredible safety record. It was just last January that the Bradley Transportation Company received the National Safety Council's Award of Honor for setting a world record in the marine transportation industry of 1000 days with no injuries.

Part of the reason for the Bradley Company's enviable record had to be luck. A ship the size of the *Carl D. Bradley* had never been lost in the Great Lakes, so maybe they pushed

The *White Rose* struck the *Bradley* near where she broke apart
Photo Credit--Father Peter Van Der Linden

her a little harder than was wise. Those who worked around her knew she had been abused and was overdue for a major refit. Even the Captain had some concern with the condition of the *Bradley* as he implied in a letter to his sister, Flora. He wrote, "This boat is getting pretty ripe for too much weather. I'll be glad when they get her fixed up." That's why we were taking her to Manitowoc. When I came aboard, I remember being told about how she was hit by the vessel *White Rose* two seasons ago, right in the area where she ripped tonight. However, the Coast Guard inspected and approved those repairs. I also recall hearing about the unexplained presence of a hairline crack that was found during drydock in Chicago over a year ago. Even so, in both 1957 & 1958, the US Coast Guard had deemed the *Carl D. Bradley* seaworthy after her annual inspections.

That wasn't all. In the spring, she damaged her bottom while leaving Cedarville, but no repairs were thought to be necessary and the incident was not reported. Earlier this month, she hit bottom again at Cedarville, and the damage, a transverse fracture about 14 inches long, was never reported. They put a "band-aid" on her, threw a couple of carriage bolts in to replace missing rivets, and sent her back out again.

31

6 *Rogers City Waits for News*

Throughout the night, Elmer would shake us and say, "Talk to me," trying to keep us from falling into a sleep from which we might not return. I'd mumble a reply, but was too exhausted to carry on a conversation. He would tell us to count out loud if we had nothing to say, but it was hard to find the energy to speak at all. He kept trying to get Gary and I to speak, but I was too busy praying. I had only attended a Catholic school in the first grade, where I received my first communion, but I had been a faithful Catholic all of my life. I found myself praying out loud, asking for the Lord's help. I'm sure Gary and Elmer were praying too.

For the most part, we just endured in silence, each man keeping to himself. I thought of my family and the families of the other crewmen, imagining what was going through their minds. The winter storm would have hit Rogers City as well, and all they could hope for was that their loved ones were in a raft or lifeboat somewhere out in the middle of the storm-lashed lake. Had they faced the unthinkable--that the men they loved and waited for were lost forever? If a storm could claim the giant *Carl D. Bradley*, what chance was there for a tiny raft or lifeboat?

Unknown to us, Elmer's "Mayday" message had created a storm of its own. One of the stations receiving it had been the marine operator in Rogers City. He had been jotting down the *Bradley's* position when Fleming's desperate call abruptly ended. He called company officials, and the word began to spread throughout the town.

32

Central Radio and Telegraph - Rogers City
Photo Credit--ML Screenings

When local TV and radio stations picked up the story, the word began to spread even more quickly. Long before the Bradley Transportation Company announced that their vessel was indeed lost, most of the families of the *Bradley* crewmen had already heard. At 7:00 PM, the company began the dreadful task of officially notifying the families of the ship's loss. They had little comfort to offer the families, since nothing was known of the fate of the crew at that time.

The telephone switchboard at Rogers City began to light up. Worried relatives called to check on their loved ones, while others called friends to inquire as to exactly who was aboard the *Bradley*. Crews from other company ships tried to call home and let their families know that they were safe and inquire about the latest news of the *Bradley*, but many of these calls could not be put through. The switchboards were overloaded, and operators were screening the calls. Some folks had to beg to get their calls put through. The demands made by the news media didn't help the situation.

Presque Isle County Advance, November 20, 1958

Friends and relatives raced to the mothers and wives of the missing crewmen, hoping to be of some help and offering their love and support. Townspeople pitched in to help their neighbors any way they could. Volunteers, like the local policeman, drove relatives to family member's houses and brought doctors to treat grieving, sometimes hysterical, people. The stress of waiting took its toll, many wives and mothers had to be sedated to help them through the ordeal.

There is a kind of kinship between sailors' wives, one that is hard to describe, especially to those that see their husbands and fathers daily. So often, their lives revolved around what time a ship was due into port. There was often only a short period of time to spend with their loved ones before the boats set sail again. A normal life was sometimes very difficult, but no one imagined life could possibly get as bad as it was that night. Sailors' wives all through the town knew if this could happen to the men on the *Bradley,* it could happen to their men. They put themselves into the shoes of the grief-stricken wives, easily envisioning what they must be going through.

34

They, probably more than anybody else, could understand the painful emotions that tore at the hearts of the wives and mothers' of the men of the *Bradley* as they waited for news. So the sailors' wives from the other Bradley ships did what they could to bring aid and comfort to their stricken sisters. In fact, so many women came to console Mary Fleming that the crowd filled her house. Together, they all listened to the local radio and television, hoping for news of their men.

The scene at Gary Strzelecki's home was being repeated at many homes throughout the area. His father, Benjamin, was completely exhausted after staying up all night trying to comfort his wife, Laverne, and daughter-in-law, Ann. He wished he had been able to convince Gary not to sail. He had hoped to team up with Gary to get an electrical contracting business going. There wouldn't have been a lot of money at first, and Benjamin knew Gary wanted to get his family on their feet. Gary took the position on the *Bradley* because it was a good paying job.

Benjamin and Laverne prayed for their son and their son in-law, Raymond Kowalski. Ray had married their daughter, Mavis, and together they had three children, Brenda, age eight, Michael, age six, and Richard, age two. Benjamin was worried about his grandchildren. Ray's father died when he was a little boy and he prayed his grandchildren would not have to grow up without a father as Ray had. Benjamin hoped for the best while preparing for the worst.

Lights burned in houses all night long in Rogers City and the nearby towns. Fathers, mothers, wives, and children all listened to WHAK "The Voice of the North", hoping for news. The station reported that other ships had joined in the search, but authorities were offering little hope of survivors considering the terrible conditions on the lake that night. Reporters repeated the same meager facts over and over as there was little news to report. The families listened anyway, and when WHAK went off the air for the night, they tuned to WSOO and listened on.

The news also spread over ship-to-ship radios as stunned crews throughout the Great Lakes listened. Could the *Carl D. Bradley* really have gone down? Some captains and mates conversed on auxiliary channels, sharing what information they had and speculating on what had happened, while others monitored channel 51 and closely followed the search efforts.

Robert Bellmore, a 27 year-old wheelsman on the *Cedarville*, was out on Lake Huron that night. His older brother, Doug, was the porter on *Carl D. Bradley,* and he was desperate for any news. Douglas and Robert were two of five brothers that sailed for the Bradley Transportation Company. Robert later said, "We heard about the disaster shortly after it happened. I knew Doug was aboard, but we couldn't get any details. Our ship was in Lake Huron and so were those of my other brothers. It was rough, but nothing like the storm on Lake Michigan." His older brother, George, a stoker on the *John G. Munson*, summed up the opinion of many when

Douglas Bellmore
Photo Credit--ML Screenings

he said, "Any boat is in trouble when the waves are running 20 to 30 feet high, like the ones reported yesterday on Lake Michigan."

During the night and into the early morning hours, the seven sons and four daughters of Myrtle Bellmore arrived at her house to console their 69-year-old mother.

Each family found their own way to deal with the waiting. Some stayed in the comfort of their homes as they waited for news, while a few made their way to the Marine Radio Station, WLC, where they stood and listened to reports from the ships and search planes. Others went to local churches to pray and to find comfort in the words of their priest or minister. Sylvester Sobeck and his wife, Cecelia went to St. Ignatius Church to pray for the safety of the *Bradley*'s crew. Sylvester had a special connection to the crew of the *Bradley*. Under ordinary circumstances, he would have been aboard the *Bradley* that night. Sylvester was her first engineer, while his nephew, George Sobeck, Jr., was the porter. They were not on the *Bradley* this trip, because George Sobeck Sr., Sylvester's brother, had passed away, and Sylvester and George Jr. were home to attend his funeral.

Sylvester and George Sobeck were not aboard
the *Bradley* on her final trip
Photo Credits--Detroit News

7 *"We Have To Go Out..."*
The Rescue Effort Begins

While Rogers City waited for news, we continued to grimly cling to the raft as it was tossed about amongst the waves. My mind wandered, and I found it hard to focus my thoughts. Was it exhaustion, hypothermia or both that was playing with my mind? I yearned for sleep and for relief from the bitter cold. There was not much more than a dull tingle in my white, lifeless-looking skin. It was as if there were a void between the surface of my skin and the nerves that lie below. Even so, I endured uncontrollable shivering accompanied by knife-like piercing pain from my cramping muscles. I knew that I dare not sleep. If I fell off the raft, I would end up like Dennis and the others. Summoning what strength I had left, I hung on.

As the night wore on, we would occasionally see red glowing lights falling from the sky. We guessed they must be flares being dropped from a plane to help illuminate the search area. Unfortunately, all the activity seemed to be south of our position. As I lay there and watched the sky light up in the distance, I found comfort in knowing they were looking for us. Elmer's message had gotten out. They were coming--it would only be a matter of time. As the endless waves pitched us about, I found the strength to hold on just a little tighter.

We didn't know the whole story until later, but the Coast Guard had been quick to respond to our call for help. Roy Brunette, station operator at WAD, the Marine Radio Station at Port Washington, Wisconsin, heard Elmer's "Mayday" message. He ordered Channel 51 cleared of all radio traffic and requested that the *Carl D. Bradley* verify its position.

Elmer had responded, "We are 12 miles southwest of Gull Island." Then he repeated his message again, "Mayday! Mayday! This is the *Carl D. Bradley*. We are 12 miles southwest of Gull Island. We are breaking in two and sinking. Any ship in the area, please come to our aid."

Roy Brunette listened carefully; he could hear voices of desperate men in the background scrambling to save their lives as their ship was going down. He felt helpless as he heard, "Mayday! May…" Then there was only the faint chatter from vessels on the Ohio and Mississippi Rivers.

His adrenaline flowing, Brunette's training kicked in. It was 17:30, almost dark. He had to get a rescue effort set in motion. He quickly contacted Coast Guard stations around the Great Lakes. Then he continued to broadcast the *Bradley's* position and requested assistance from any vessel in the area.

At 17:40, Roy Brunette assumed radio control of channel 51 and declared a Search And Rescue Emergency. He then broadcast an order for radio silence. This order was broadcast by station WAD several times, and repeated by many other mid-eastern radio stations. However, there was still some interference from the unauthorized use of channel 51 by a few boats on the Great Lakes, the Ohio and Mississippi Rivers and radio stations around the Midwest.

Elmer's "Mayday" message was heard by a large number of marine radio stations, freighters and "ham" radio operators. The captain of the *SS Robert C. Stanley* heard the "Mayday" and readied his ship to assist. Sheltering from the storm behind Garden Island, she raised her anchors and joined the search less than an hour after she heard the call. The *Elton*

Hoyt II was also in the area and changed course to assist in the effort. The Plum Island Lifeboat Station reported the distress call and dispatched *CG-40300*, a small Coast Guard boat. The Coast Guardsmen made a valiant effort, but had to turn back, because they were unable to make headway against the towering seas.

DISASTER STRIKES
NOVEMBER 18, 1958 – TIME - 5:28 P. M.

Rogers City was stunned by the news that the Str. Carl D. Bradley had broken in two and sank in the waters of Lake Michigan. The Bradley went to the bottom within minutes after sending a "May Day" distress signal at 5:28 p.m.

A voice over the ship to shore telephone said: "We've broken in half, We're going down." That was the word that shocked a community that derived a great portion of its livelihood from its maritime operations. It had never happened before. Ships would come and ships would go, and the men who sailed them had always come home. Friends at home waited anxiously throughout the long night, hoping and praying that they would return again.

The Str. Cedarville lies at dock at the Port of Calcite next to the empty berth where the Carl D. Bradley was to tie up at 2:00 a.m. Wednesday morning.

Presque Isle County Advance, November 27, 1958

In the Ninth District Coast Guard Rescue Coordination Center in Cleveland, officers were reviewing the available ships and aircraft that could be used in the search. The USCG Cutter *Hollyhock*, based in Sturgeon Bay, Wisconsin was on two-hour recall status and could be sent across the lake. There was a small lifeboat on Beaver Island, but it had an inexperienced crew and, with the size of the waves, it would be of little help. Of the two Coast Guard planes stationed at Traverse City, Michigan, one was down for maintenance, while the other was returning from an air search in southern

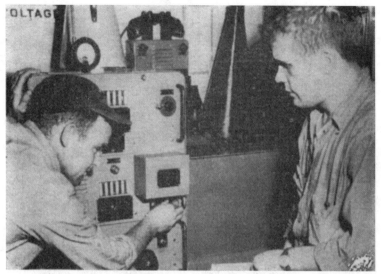

The "Mayday" message is received in Charlevoix
Photo Credit--Detroit Free Press

Lake Michigan. That aircraft, callsign UF 1273, was directed to the scene. As an amphibian, it could be used to search, but there was no possibility of attempting a water landing if survivors were spotted. The lake was just too rough. In addition to the planes, there were three helicopters stationed in Traverse City, but with wind gusts reported over 65 miles per hour, it was deemed unsafe to dispatch them. Their crews waited in readiness throughout the long night.

In Charlevoix, the "Mayday" message was received by the USCG Lifeboat Station. They, in turn, passed it on to Lieutenant Commander Harold Muth, captain of the USCG Cutter *Sundew*, which was stationed there.

The *Sundew's* normal in-port status was termed Bravo 2, which meant they were to respond to any search and rescue calls within two hours or less. However, on this particular day, the *Sundew* was in Charlie 12 status, which meant they had authorization to do minor repairs on the main engines, but must be able to get underway in answer to a search and rescue call within 12 hours.

Captain Harold Muth, USCG
Photo Credit--ML Screenings

Captain Muth recalls that phone call and the events that followed:

Sometime shortly after 5:30 in the evening of November 18, 1958, I received a call at home from the Charlevoix Lifeboat Station, advising that the *Carl D. Bradley* had broken up and apparently sank in a storm in Northern Lake Michigan. I quickly explained to my wife, Doloras, what had happened. Just two days earlier, she had come home from the hospital after giving birth to our son, Harold. Without complaint, she handed me my hat, kissed me goodbye, and I was on my way to the *Sundew*, arriving there some five or six minutes later.

The crew had already started taking measures to prepare the *Sundew* for heavy weather. This meant placing ashore the

42

The USCGC *Sundew* at Charlevoix
Photo Credit--Robert Fitz

heavy equipment that we used in servicing aids to navigation and pumping water into two empty fuel tanks in the forward part of the ship to improve our ballast condition. In addition, we lashed down anything that could possibly come loose. I soon realized that I was not going to get the entire crew back because of our recall status. When my executive officer informed me that they had enough men to stand the watches and, of considerable importance, that we had a cook and a hospital corpsman aboard, I gave the order to depart. I had a good crew, and we were able to get underway in about 45 minutes.

Earlier that day, Warren Toussaint, the hospital corpsman, had been on duty as the Master Of Arms. Despite the fact that they were in port, he had to remain aboard until everybody had been fed. Around 5:00 PM, he was relieved of duty and left the ship. Toussaint recalled what happened as he arrived home:

I had just sat down to dinner when the telephone call came from the executive officer, telling me to get back aboard the ship. We had a mission, and the captain didn't want to sail without me. I lived on the east side of town, only about eight blocks away from the *Sundew's* mooring.

My wife, Norma, drove me down to the ship, which gave me time to get my wits about me. Our three children, Dale, Cary and Deborah, were sitting quietly in the back seat. While driving Norma asked, "Are you really going out in this?"

I replied, "You got to go, Norma. You got to go." As we drove, an old unofficial Coast Guard motto came to mind, "You have to go out, but you don't have to come back." I told my wife, "Now, there's one thing I want to tell you honey. If anything happens to me, don't believe anything you hear on the news. You wait until a Coast Guard Officer stands at the front door and says your husband is dead. Then you can believe it."

She quietly answered, " I know that."

"The metal box has the insurance papers," I reminded her.

"I know that," she murmured and that is all she said.

There wasn't even time for kisses goodbye, because the ship's engines were already warming up and the mooring lines were singled. I jumped out of the car and heard the captain on the deck shouting, "Hurry up, hurry up! We have to get going." There were some guys behind me, but that's how fast it happened.

The *Sundew* was normally moored facing southeastward, about 100 feet from the old railroad bridge, so to leave port, the vessel had to be turned around. The regular routine was to go through the railroad bridge, turn the ship around in Lake Charlevoix and come back through the railroad bridge, which was almost always open. We'd then continue through Round

Lake, through the highway bridge and out the channel into Lake Michigan.

This particular evening, we left dock and went through the railroad bridge. We proceeded into Lake Charlevoix okay, but at first, we couldn't get back out through the railroad bridge.

I heard Captain Muth say, "Standby! We're getting out of here." He couldn't hit the bridge opening head on because of the wind, so he steered the ship towards the southwest side of the channel and gunned it. He let the storm assist us right through the bridge. It was almost a miracle that the ship never touched either side of it. Once we got through the bridge, we were in the lee of the land, because Round Lake is surrounded with hills.

When we went through the railroad bridge, I remember looking up, seeing my wife and children and thinking to myself, "I may never see them again." By the time the *Sundew* got to the highway bridge, half of the city was waiting for us. The word was out. The *Sundew* was going to try to rescue the crew of the *Bradley*.

* * *

As the *Sundew* was getting underway, the special sea detail took their places on the buoy deck and the bow. On a ship of the *Sundew's* class, the buoy deck is forward of the bridge, just behind the bow of the ship. It is seven or eight feet below the weather deck with about five or six feet of freeboard above the water. The large boom that was used to set buoys in the water was located here, although, the buoys themselves had been offloaded to prepare the ship for heavy seas. If survivors were recovered, this is where they would be brought aboard.

Robert Fitz on the *Sundew's* bow

Two sailors stood lookout in the bow of the ship, while Damage Controlman Robert Fitz took position next to the anchor brake control. It would be his job to release the anchor if the Sundew had to make an emergency stop. As the Sundew passed through the highway bridge, Fitz looked up at the townspeople waiting there to see them off. Standing just a little straighter, he felt pride in what his ship was going to try to do. Fitz remembers thinking:

This is exactly why I went into the Coast Guard. Being a farmer, I didn't want to go into a branch of service that took lives. I wanted to save lives. I hoped that tonight I would play a part in saving someone's life.

My wife, Mary Ann would worry though. I think it's harder on the wives than on the guys who are actually out there. The mind is capable of imagining some pretty awful things, and they had lots of time to think while we were at sea. I think some of the wives might have actually been worried that we might not come back.

46

Hopefully Mary Ann would find some comfort listening to our Hallicrafter's shortwave radio. I had owned it since high school and enjoyed scanning the airwaves. In all likelihood, other wives would join her in our apartment on Charlevoix Street, and together, they would listen to the radio chatter and reassure each other that their men would come back safe.

For myself, I had complete faith in the Coast Guard and in my captain. I knew there was danger, but I wasn't worried. Our mission today was just part of the job. We were doing what we trained for.

That night was as bad as I'd ever seen it, very wet and cold. When I joined the Coast Guard, I discovered that I had a tendency to get seasick, but there was nothing I could do about it now. The roar of the engines combined with the howling wind and crashing waves meant I had to wear earphones in order to receive messages from the bridge. What struck me was, with all of the other noise, I could hear the whine of the anemometer. Even though the wind speed indicator was located far above, I could hear its piercing, sharp whine above everything else.

The real problem was the wind, the sleet, and the bitter cold. It chilled us to the bone. I longed to get out of the storm, but it was my duty to stay at my post until relieved.

* * *

As the *Sundew* went through the narrow channel into Lake Michigan, it was rolling heavily from the force of the wind. As she passed the Coast Guard Lifeboat Station, just a short distance from the end of the channel, the men on deck were relieved of their sea duty and came in. They were the last men that would be allowed on the exposed deck that night. Robert Fitz went to his quarters, changed into dry clothes, and crawled into his bunk. Even wrapped in several layers of blankets, he could not get warm.

On the navigation bridge, Warrant Boatswain Jack (John) Coppens was at his station next to the gyro compass. Coppens remembers the Sundew's departure from Charlevoix:

It was blowing like Hell as we headed out into the lake. We had set a special sea detail for leaving our moorings, but as soon as we went through the piers, it was evident nobody could stay on deck. We brought everyone inside, it was just too rough. As soon as we got outside the point of Charlevoix, I remember the ship starting to roll heavily from side to side and the wind making a shrieking sound as it went through the rigging. The way the boat was rolling, you had to wonder if she was going to come back, but after about 50 times of that you would say, "Well, this is a pretty good ship. I don't think she's going to roll!"

* * *

Soon after clearing the breakwall, the *Sundew* encountered the *CG-36392*, a 36-foot motor lifeboat that had been launched by the Charlevoix lifeboat station. This small vessel was having problems with her steering and was unable to hold to a course in the battering seas.

Captain Muth remembers:

I saw the lifeboat struggling to make headway and not wishing to have a second problem on my hands, I advised them to return to port. They gave it a good try, but I imagine they were pretty glad to get back to port and out of the storm.

The winds were 50 to 55 MPH with occasional gusts to 65 MPH, and the forecast called for some strengthening of the storm. The best position we had on the sinking of the *Bradley* was approximately ten miles southwest of Gull Island. This was 45 miles distant from Charlevoix, and we were only able to do about ten miles per hour. Our course to that position was 300 degrees true. This course put us in the trough of the seas, and we experienced some very heavy rolling, sometimes 30 to 35 degrees.

The 36-foot motor lifeboat attempts to join the rescue mission
Photo Credit--US Coast Guard

I hadn't encountered seas this bad since I was on North Atlantic convoy duty during World War II. Every once in a while, we would get knocked over 30 degrees or so, and a second wave would hit us before we could recover. The *Sundew* would then roll to about 50 degrees. A couple of times, we rolled to 55 degrees. Every five minutes or so, you would get two big waves together, the "Two Sisters", as they are called on the Great Lakes, and they would really knock us down. The waves that night ran anywhere from 25 to 30 feet, and I would say these two big waves were probably 10 to 15 feet higher than that. Such waves usually came in pairs or sometimes in threes. That night, I only remember them in pairs, because the first one would roll you over and knock you down, and then as you came up, before you could even get upright, the second wave would hit and the ship would really heel over.

Throughout the night, we kept people off the exposed decks, because there was just too much green water coming aboard, especially on the buoy deck. As the *Sundew* would meet a wave, a solid wall of water would roll across the buoy deck and crash against the superstructure. In fact, that is how we lost our main radio transmitter. The main intake for the ventilation system was just behind the wheelhouse, about 25 to 30 feet above the water. Since we were hitting the waves at an angle and rolling heavily, we managed to roll into an oncoming wave and take water directly down the ventilator. Before we knew what had happened, we had water sloshing around in the radio room, and our main transmitter was shorted out.

I asked the chief electrician's mate to come up to see if he could rectify the situation. He arrived shortly and went inside to see what he could do. I didn't hear from him for five to ten minutes, so I went back to the radio room to check on him. I found him perched on top of the chart desk, surrounded by about eight inches of water that was sloshing back and forth on the deck. From his position on the chart desk, he told me that the main transmitter was blown beyond repair and that, if we were lucky, the secondary transmitter would survive, which it did. It was a comical sight, because lake water had gotten into some soap powder that we stored in a little cleaning locker in the radio shack. The soapy mixture sloshing back and forth had created quite a frothy mess.

As if the shorted out transmitter wasn't bad enough, we also received a report from our engine room that water was coming down the stack, the top of which was a good 35 feet above the water line. The water was threatening our main electrical switchboard. This was dangerous, because the *Sundew* is a diesel electric boat. Two big diesel generators drove a large electric motor, which turned the propeller shaft. The water had splashed all over the main board, and the engineers were afraid that we were going to lose our power. They asked me to be careful. I said, "Well, we're just trying to keep the ship afloat and get it out to where we're suppose to be."

Rolling and pitching through the heavy seas, the *Sundew* finally arrived at the search area about 22:45, or 10:45 PM. We commenced our search using the ship's searchlight. We could never see beyond the next wave, a distance of only 75 to 100 feet.

While enroute to the *Bradley's* last reported position, I had an occasion to talk to the motor vessel, *Christian Sartori*, a 254-foot German ship that was on her way to Chicago. She had been the first vessel reach the search area.

* * *

Although the *Christian Sartori's* crew did not hear Fleming's "Mayday" call, lookouts on her deck watched as the lights went out on the *Bradley's* forward section, and later saw the explosion as her stern slipped beneath the waves. A check of the *Sartori's* radar screen showed the *Bradley* was gone.

The *Christian Sartori* was approximately five miles from the *Bradley* at the time of the sinking, and it took the *Sartori* an hour and a half to reach that position. The *Sartori's* captain, Paul Mueller, gave the position of the sinking as five to six miles northwest of Boulder Reef. Captain Mueller also reported that his crew had seen flares on the water nearly an hour after the *Bradley* sank. Upon arriving at the site, the *Christian Sartori* saw only a large tank and a floating raincoat. They saw nothing else in the way of wreckage.

USCGC *Hollyhock*
Photo Credit--Ralph Roberts

Captain Muth recalls his conversation with Captain Mueller that night:

I contacted the *Christian Sartori* on the radio and asked them to remain on the scene until we arrived there. Captain Mueller had told me that they were on a tight schedule; they had to get to Chicago and back out to the Saint Lawrence Seaway before the Seaway closed, which was in early December. He was up against a time element. I asked if he would remain on scene until I arrived, and Captain Mueller said he would.

Captain Paul Mueller
Photo Credit--Detroit Times

When I arrived on scene, Captain Mueller asked to be released, and I asked him if he would stay for another hour or two until the arrival of the Coast Guard Cutter *Hollyhock*, which was coming up from Sturgeon Bay, Wisconsin. I told him if he would remain with me, searching the area just northeast of the sinking until the *Hollyhock* arrived, I would much appreciate it. Captain Mueller voiced some concern again about his schedule, but said yes, he would do that.

At one point, I asked Captain Mueller if he would stay just one more half hour, and when that half hour was up, I asked him if he would extend that half hour for another half hour. He thought I was playing games with him. But he stuck it out. He did a real good job. Like a good skipper, Captain Mueller stayed until 1:30 that morning when *Hollyhock* arrived. He left at that point with our blessing.

The *SS Robert C. Stanley*, an ore boat, joined us around this time. At that point, the seas were averaging 25 feet and the winds had picked up to 65 MPH with occasional gusts to 70. In an attempt to cut down on the heavy rolling and pitching,

I found it necessary to put the seas on our port bow on the outbound search legs, and on the return leg, to put the seas on our starboard quarter. This allowed us to do a better job of lookout work. As a result, our search directions were pretty much east and west across the anticipated drift line where we thought that any wreckage would be found. We searched the area northeast of the sinking for five to ten miles along this drift line with no results.

The crew on the *Sundew* was short-handed, so people had to perform duties that they normally didn't do. Such as cooks being helmsmen and lookouts, others being searchlight operators. The hospital corpsman, Warren Toussaint, spent several hours manning the searchlight.

Toussaint recalls the terror of that night:

To say that the storm was intimidating would be an understatement. Was I scared? You're darn right I was scared. Everybody was. Anybody that was not scared was nuts. None of the crew would go down below to sleep. Most of them wouldn't even go down to their quarters, which is one deck below the main deck. About once an hour, the captain would tell me to take a look around and check on the guys, which on a normal day would take about 30 seconds. With the ship rolling the way she was, it took more like 15 minutes. Going down the ladder was slow, as I had to take it one careful step at a time. At all times, I had to hold on, otherwise I could have been thrown to the deck and broke my arm or otherwise been injured. Once I got on the main deck, I had to move one foot at a time. I didn't walk, I just grabbed from side to side. The guys in the mess hall had tied themselves to the mess table. They were loose knots. But what they didn't realize is that, if the ship rolled over, they wouldn't have had a chance.

I went to the stern of the ship, where I encountered one crewman with his backside against one side of the passageway and his two hands pressed against the other. He was just trying to stay in place. He was looking a little green, and his eyes asked the question we all were all thinking, "Are we going to make it?"

Two passageways run aft, one on either side of the ship. You can access the engine room from either one by taking a ladder that went straight down into the engine spaces. I went down a little ways until I spotted Chief Gallagher standing by the ladder below me. He had been born and raised on nearby Beaver Island and knew how treacherous these waters could be. He had his two hands on the ladder and was looking up at the inclinometer, the device that tells the tilt of the ship. There is an arrow on it that hangs straight down at zero. As the ship rolls, the arrow stays straight down, and it registers how many degrees the ship has rolled to port or starboard. I said, "What's the matter Chief?"

He said, "If that thing hits 60 degrees I'm out of here." Jim Gallagher had been on the Murmansk Run in World War II, so he was no amateur. He knew what he was talking about.

I said, "I'll be right behind you."

He quickly replied, " You had better be, or else you ain't gonna' get out of this place."

Robert Fitz remembers the seemingly endless night as the Sundew *rolled and pitched in the angry seas:*

Because the captain would want the ship to be on a even keel as much as possible, one of my jobs was to keep the ship trimmed at all times while in good weather. Sometimes, I did that by pumping diesel fuel or water ballast from port tanks to starboard tanks, but in a storm, you can't do that. During the storm, I was well aware of the *Sundew's* list, because that was something I had to watch every single day.

Another one of my jobs was damage repair. I had a workshop down below by the engine room where I did welding. Unfortunately, I did not secure all the drawers in my workbench before we left Charlevoix. The bench had something like a flat washer welded to each drawer. When these washers were all lined up, a steel rod was shoved down through the holes, and this secured all the drawers from coming out. That is the standard procedure when they say to secure the ship for heavy seas. For whatever reason, I didn't do it. After we got underway, things really got noisy with all the stuff slam banging around. Those drawers came out and what a mess I had.

Wherever you were in the ship, you were bombarded with noise. You heard everything that wasn't bolted down as it slammed around. Even up topside, anything that hadn't been secured really tight was being tossed around. The *Sundew* was carrying about 50 large tanks of acetylene gas on the deck for the buoys, and hadn't had time to offload them before leaving. About half of them broke free and went over the side. It was total pandemonium.

The constant, violent motions of the ship made matters difficult for everyone. We didn't walk, we lurched, grabbing onto whatever was available. It was a waste of time to try to repair anything, so I retired to my quarters.

I spent most of the night in my bunk. There certainly wasn't any sleeping. I don't think anybody slept that night. I wasn't afraid; I had complete trust in the Coast Guard and my ship. I'd be lying if I said I wasn't seasick, but I wasn't afraid. For once, I wasn't embarrassed by my seasickness, because I certainly wasn't the only one. Lots of people were seasick, officers and enlisted men alike.

They say that storms on the Great Lakes are rougher than on the ocean, and I believe it. As we fought our way through the storm that night, our bow would be way, way down when the next wave would appear as a huge wall of water that would bury the ship. For a moment, you felt like you were on a submarine, then the mass of water would rush to the scuppers, where it escaped out of the sides of the ship. A moment later, we'd be way the heck up high on the wave's crest, and then, it started over again. It was just up and down for hour after hour. Don't forget that, during all this time, the ship was also rolling violently from port to starboard and back. Throw in the howl of the raging wind, the freezing rain pounding against the ship, the clatter of loose objects slamming about, and you have a little idea what it was like. Through all of this, we could hear the steady sound of the diesel engines down below. It was a reassuring sound, because it meant that we were still in control and moving forward.

8 What Brought Me to this Place? Frank's Story Continues...

I didn't know the men who were risking their lives to come to my rescue, but I was comforted to know that they were out there looking. I just hoped that they would find us in time. Elmer lay across from me, looking so cold and pale. I wondered what he would give for a cup of warm coffee now? Hoping to avoid an earache, I shoved the corner of my collar into my ear and tried to block the wind. Then, I noticed that the water on my hair was starting to freeze solid. I felt a moment of fear. What if I became encased in ice before dawn? I tried not to think of it. I let my mind wander back through the events that had brought me to this time and place.

When I took up sailing, I never dreamed that anything like this would happen. I guess sailing was just the natural thing for me to do. I have always been adventurous, and sailing seemed like it would offer more excitement than a factory job. I remembered back to high school, to the time just before we graduated, when we had what was called a skip day. That was a day that all the seniors would go somewhere. Bernard Bader and I took off on a Thursday night and went to Cleveland. I had a car then, so first we went to Detroit. Then we went to Toledo. I said, "What the heck. Let's go all the way to Cleveland." When we came back to school, the principal, Harry Grambau, was a bit upset. He said, "You only get one day off, not two."

I said, "But we went to Cleveland."

Frank at graduation
Photo credit--Frank Mays

I got my sailing card in the spring of that same year. I went to see a Mr. Jones, and he gave me a slip that said the Bradley Transportation Company was going to hire Frank Mays when he graduates. With these papers and birth certificate in hand, I went up to St. Ignace to the Coast Guard Station, and they issued me my sailing card.

A funny thing happened when I went to get my birth certificate for my sailing card. The county clerk at that time was Renatta Getzinger. I distinctly remember that day, because when Mrs. Getzinger came out with my birth certificate, my name was spelled wrong. My last name was Mayes and it was on my birth certificate as Mays. I said, "That's not right."

She said, "Yes it is!" and she brought out the big book. Here it was in Dr. Arscott's handwriting. I was recorded as being born on November 24, 1931 at 8:20 AM as Frank Louis Mays. He had made a mistake. My family didn't know this and neither did I. My high school diploma and other documents were in the name of Frank Mayes.

Frank Mays as a young man in 1952

Mrs. Getzinger said it would cost between 60 and 70 dollars to get the paper work done to change the birth certificate. I didn't have the money, my parents didn't either, and before I knew it, there I was with a sailing card with a different name on it.

I've never been in the habit of sitting still too long. I graduated in June of 1950, on a Tuesday, and the following Thursday, I had a job aboard the steamer *Adam E. Cornelius* and was on my way. The "Bradley Boats" would hire you out of the office, but any outside boats that came in would hire you on the spot. So when the *Adam E. Cornelius* came into port, I went down to the dock and went aboard. I asked the second mate if they needed anybody on board.

He said, "Yah, they need a deck hand. Go and see the first mate, Juba.

His name was Leo Nowaczewski and he was from Alpena. His nickname was "Juba."

When I found Juba, he asked, "You got a sailing card?"

I replied, "Yes."

He said, "Okay, then go see the clerk, you're hired." Just like that, I had a job. I went home. My bags had been packed all of this time. I threw my bag on my back and told my parents, "I'm going on the *Adam E. Cornelius* as a deckhand. Goodbye."

On my first trip, we left Calcite and went to Buffalo, New York, with a load of stone. We followed up that voyage with several trips in Lake Erie running cargo between the ports there.

I remember when we went through the Welland Canal into Lake Ontario then up to Montreal. Boy, I thought that was fun. I had never been that far from Rogers City in my life. That was the only trip that I sailed on Lake Ontario. I had a lot of fun that year. In December of 1950, I laid the *Cornelius* up in Manitowoc, Wisconsin. I remember having a friend, Jimmy Smith, drive my car to Manitowoc, and then he took a bus back home, leaving the car for me. When I finished up in December, I began my drive back home, making stops along the way. I remember stopping in Chicago and seeing my aunt, my dad's sister, before I went back home to Rogers City.

In January of 1951, I went to Detroit to work at a little manufacturing company that made small industrial transmissions that a jeweler might use. I didn't stay there long, because on February 21st, I joined the Navy. I took my boot camp at the Great Lakes Naval Training Center, and then I was transferred to a auxiliary air station in Philadelphia called Henry C. Mustin Field. I was there when I was accepted to Personnelman School in Bainbridge, Maryland. After my training was completed, I was granted three years of shore duty, which I spent at Mustin Field. Once my shore duty expired, I was transferred to the destroyer *USS Johnston DD 821*, stationed at Newport, Rhode Island. She was the second ship to bear the name *Johnston*, the first having sunk in the south Pacific during the Second World War. I left the Navy after completing a four-year tour.

Yeah, I saw some rough seas during my time in the Navy, but nothing compared to what I experienced that last night on the *Bradley*. As the relentless waves tossed the raft around, I hung on for my life, and my thoughts returned to the *Bradley*. I prayed that there would be other survivors. We had a good crew aboard the *Bradley*, and I knew all of them one way or another.

My closest friends aboard the ship were those men on my watch. We worked with each other every day and became a team. There was a saying on board that was often heard if it was close to quitting time, "Ah, leave it for the next watch." Even so, when they really needed a hand, we would stay on. We always helped each other out. We all got along. I guess we had to. We had nowhere else to go.

Sailors have a reputation for being big drinkers, but that really wasn't true in our case. We didn't go to bars together much at all. You know, when you first start sailing, you think it would be fun until you get into port and find out how far you have to walk from the unloading docks to the nearest bar. That doesn't mean we never went into a bar together when we arrived in port. I remember when I was on the steamer *Rogers*

Most of the *Bradley's* crew was from the Rogers City area
Photo credit--ML Screenings

City in 1957; we would haul clinkers from one cement plant near Gary, Indiana, to another cement plant in Milwaukee. They would swing the boom out to unload the ship, and right at the end of the boom was a bar. So, we would go relax in there. Once in a while, the captain would join us for a social drink. We would sit and relax, while someone kept watch out the window. When he saw them swing the unloading boom back toward the ship, he would yell, "Okay, we got to go now." Reluctantly, we would all head back to the ship.

Usually though, if you wanted something to drink, you would have your wife or someone else purchase the alcohol in Rogers City, because we were there every three or four days. If you really needed something while on board the ship, there were always the "Bum Boats." These small boats would have a little store below deck. As they came alongside of the freighters, sailors would go aboard and buy toiletries, shaving lotion, newspapers, and items like that.

Aboard the *Bradley*, I knew the people up forward better than those in the aft section because I associated with them more. We'd put a card table in the companionway just outside of our cabins, and each guy would grab a chair from his room. We would play poker, of course, but a popular game around the Rogers City area was called spitzer. I learned to play spitzer and pinochle on the boats, because the crew played them a lot and they were good pastimes. Some of the guys would play for money, but I only got into those games when we played for 50 cent pieces and there was a given limit.

It was different when I sailed on the *Adam E. Cornelius*. We were paid in cash, and most of the guys blew their whole paycheck playing cards. On the *Cornelius*, there were a lot of single guys. We had a big game room with a round table and a lamp over it. I didn't get into those games, though. When I got paid, I would leave all but $20 in the clerk's safe until I arrived home in Rogers City.

We got paid once a month on the *Cornelius*, but you could make a draw twice a month. A lot of guys would make a draw just to play poker. They would draw $20 out, and if they lost it, well fine. But a few guys would keep drawing it. I guess it all depends on their personality. A few guys made a lot of money playing cards, but most were lucky that the job included free room and board.

The crews of the "Bradley Boats" I sailed on played a lot of poker, but there were never high stakes. Our guys were primarily family men and college kids who needed their dollars.

There was a funny thing about the *Bradley*. You could leave money lying around and it wouldn't be touched, but if you left reading material out, it would disappear quickly. That's how Dick Book and I became friends. I would go into his cabin and borrow something to read. We would chitchat about people and places we knew in Waterloo, Iowa and Cedar Rapids.

Richard J. Book
Photo Credit--ML Screenings

I used to joke with him, asking, "What is a boy from Iowa doing on the Great Lakes?"

He would always respond with, "What was a guy from the Great Lakes doing in Iowa?"

I would come back with, "I married a girl from Iowa, what's your excuse?"

Did I forget to mention that I was married? While I was in the Navy, I met Marlys Bush from Waterloo, Iowa. I met her through her uncle, who I served with in the Navy. We had leave one time and didn't know where to go, so he said,

"Come on let's go out to Minnesota and see my family," and so I did.

Marlys and I got married in October of 1953. While I was in the Navy, we had one son, Michael. When I was discharged, I went back out to Waterloo, Iowa, where I got a job with the John Deere Tractor Company, working in the machine shop. I didn't like that job at all, so I quit and got a job selling Wonder Bread. I was working at that job when, on July 30, 1956, our second son, Mark, was born.

One day, I was out driving my bread truck, and I cut it too close while crossing in front of a train. Imagine my surprise when the train rammed into the backside of the bread truck. I didn't get hurt, but the truck got pretty well demolished. That's why I left the bread company.

I took a job in Waterloo working for a beer distributor, where I sold *Miller High Life* for awhile. I didn't care for that job either, so when I got word that U.S. Steel was hiring sailors, we packed up the two boys and went to live in Rogers City, Michigan. My hometown became the birthplace of my third son, Frank.

I guess I had always been a sailor at heart. It was hard to grow up in Rogers City without sailing getting into your blood. I was always restless; I guess I took after my brothers.

Frank, with his older brothers, Lloyd and Harry

Photo credit--Frank Mays

Harry, my oldest brother, started sailing on the Great Lakes at the age of 16. When the war broke out, he got off the Great Lakes' boats and enlisted into the merchant marine for ocean duty. He sailed for a period of time, then attended the Maritime Academy in Sheepshead Bay, New York. He graduated as an engineer and sailed on ocean vessels throughout the war. When the war was over, he came back and sailed on the Great Lakes for a while. It wasn't too long before he got bored and enlisted in the army as a paratrooper. After he was discharged, he returned to Great Lakes and sailed for the Ford Motor Company as an engineer.

Lloyd was two years older than I was. He started sailing in the summer months when he was still in high school. He graduated in 1948 and continued work on various boats for the next two years. He moved to Detroit around 1950. I remember visiting him there just before I went into the Navy. He enlisted in the Air Force for a couple of years. When he was discharged, he went back to sailing with the Bradley Fleet.

Frank's parents,
Mary and Frank Mayes
in Rogers City

Photo credit--Frank Mays

I don't know where my brothers and I got the desire to travel and sail. My father sailed for one summer as a young man, but he didn't like it. For 47 years, he worked as a millwright for the Michigan Lime and Chemical Company at Rogers City. They operate the largest limestone quarry in the world.

We didn't get the desire to sail from our grandparents either, although we probably got our spirit of adventure from them. They were homesteaders. My father's father, Thomas, came from East Prussia with his two sisters in the 1800s and landed in Baltimore, Maryland. One sister went to the Chicago area, and one sister went to Detroit. Thomas went up to the Rogers City area to claim some land for himself around the small town of Posen. He married and had ten children. He died when my father was about a year old and my grandmother was expecting with his little sister. My grandmother later remarried and had two more sons.

My mother's father sailed by freighter from Milwaukee, Wisconsin to claim his land. He met my grandmother in Posen, and they got married. They settled in the Posen/Metz area and had seven children.

I started to think about my mother. How would she be taking the news? Had she given up on me? If I can just make it 'til daylight...

9 *Dawn Breaks - It's Now or Never*

In the early morning hours of November nineteenth, the men on the bridge of the *Sundew* were pretty much exhausted. Their muscles ached from having to hang on tight to keep from being thrown about. At this time, Captain Muth decided to relieve hospital corpsman, Warren Toussaint, who was operating the searchlight and send him down to get some rest. Without having to be told, Toussaint knew that the skipper wanted him rested so he would be prepared to deal with any survivors or bodies that they might find in the morning. As Toussaint went below, Captain Muth returned his attention to the search for the *Bradley's* crew.

Captain Muth remembers seeing what appeared to be a lifejacket:

We turned the ship around to try to pick it up, but we were unable to relocate it. It was hard for the searchlight to penetrate the spray, so we could only see as far as the next wave. The waves acted like walls of water, and only when we rose to the crests were we able to see any distance at all.

We searched all night, as did the *Hollyhock*, *Holt* and *Stanley*, yet found nothing. At four in the morning, I asked the *Stanley* and the *Hollyhock* to continue to search just northwest of Gull Island while I checked out a different area. Acting on a hunch, I took the *Sundew* up to a point west of Trout Island in the possibility that some of the wreckage had gone by us in the darkness. Searching up in that area provided no results either. The Coast Guard aircraft on the scene dropped over

70

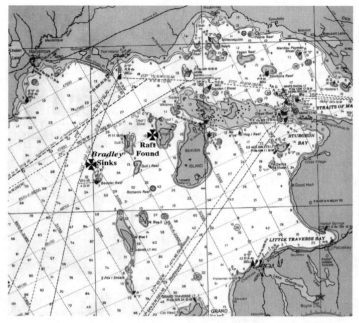

Chart showing where the *Bradley* sank and the raft was recovered

100 flares but they were not much help to us because of the limited visibility conditions.

Other lake vessels were arriving on the scene, and as each checked in, I assigned them an area to search. Surely the *Bradley* had not disappeared without a trace. One of us had to get lucky soon.

Around six in the morning, I decided to try a new approach. Perhaps some of the wreckage, or maybe even a lifeboat or life raft might have drifted to the south of Gull Island. I decided to take the *Sundew* and search the area between Gull Island and High Island.

Back on the raft, Frank, Gary and Elmer await the coming of the morning light. Frank recalls:

It seemed like we had been on the raft for days instead of hours. Even though I had my watch in my pocket, I had no way of telling what time it was as it was just too dark. Elmer and I had managed to stay awake, but I feared Gary had fallen asleep.

As a little light began to penetrate the darkness, we could almost tell the water from the sky, Gary started to stir, but it wasn't the Gary we knew. He had a blank stare, and there was some foam in the corners of his mouth. Elmer and I tried to speak to him, but he didn't reply. He seemed to be delirious, which I later learned can be one of the symptoms of severe hypothermia. All at once, he began to crawl with a swimming motion toward the edge of the raft. Elmer and I grabbed him and desperately tried to keep him on board, but he broke free. We caught him again, but it was as though he had found a new source of energy. In our weakened condition, he broke free of our grasp and slid into the water.

He swam off into the dim light; we strained our eyes to keep track of him, but he was quickly gone from sight. One moment we saw him, the next moment he was gone. In his mind, was he swimming to safety, or was he off to rescue his brother-in-law, Ray? Even though we knew Gary was an excellent swimmer, we didn't hold out much hope for him. With every hour that passed, we knew our own chances of survival were getting less and less.

Saddened by my inability to help Gary, I lay down again. As I clung to the raft, I noticed that the waves were not quite as big and that the wind had slackened a bit. The sky was lighting up, and dawn was coming. This brought renewed hope. Surely they should be able to see us now.

I was startled from my reverie when Elmer shouted, "I see something." I figured it was probably only a seagull, but even a live seagull would be worth looking at. There, in distance, was a plane. Although it was not too close, we could clearly make it out. They must see us, I thought. We began imagining that they were calling in our location right now. The thought never occurred to us to question why they hadn't flown over to take a closer look and circled us a couple of times. I guess our minds were not prepared to accept the possibility that rescue could come so near and then turn away again. We took comfort in the hope that they had found us, even if that was not the case.

I stared at the eastern horizon as the darkness lifted and an orange glow began to filter through the clouds. Suddenly, I realized that in the distance was the silhouette of what appeared to be land. I yelled to Elmer, "Look there's an island over there." Elmer said, "That has to be High Island, because I have Trout Island on this side. I turned to where Elmer was looking, and sure enough, there was a smaller island behind me. I was impressed with Elmer's knowledge of the lakes and his navigational skill.

You can't imagine my excitement at being so close to land. It was about 60 yards away. I could make out the shape of trees in the dim light. The lake was calmer near the island, because we were more protected. Elmer did not seem as excited as I was. He said, "You know, at the speed we're drifting, we'll probably float right back into the open water."

I couldn't take that. That was the last straw. "You know, Elmer, we could swim over to the islands, and we could build a signal fire." I knew I wasn't being realistic. We didn't have matches, and our muscles were so exhausted that it was a struggle just to lift our heads. Could I really swim that far?

I yearned to be on dry land, off of this small raft, away from the waves and the tormenting spray.

Cold water splashing me in the face brought me back to reality. We would have to stick with the raft. Giving our tiny perch a quick look over, I noticed with alarm that the sea anchor was gone. Somehow, during the night, it had come off. Had the rope frayed or the knot come loose? It didn't make any difference. Once again, we were at the mercy of the waves.

The sky was noticeably brighter, and we were able to see much further. I had kept my spirits up by telling myself that I only had to hold on 'til daylight, but where was our rescue? Just then, Elmer yelled, "There's a boat out there." I quickly turned to where he was looking. On the horizon, I could see a black ship in the distance. As we watched it grow, our hearts

The Coast Guard Cutter *Sundew*
Photo Credit--Ralph Roberts

swelled with hope, and for a brief moment, we forgot about the night of cold, pain and death. We imaged the warmth we would find on board this ship, which was coming directly at us. Could they really see us? The closer it came, the more detail I could make out. White upperworks, a black hull with big white numbers on it--it had to be the Coast Guard!

I stared at the sky as the sun broke over the horizon and shone its amber light through the thick cloud cover. I whispered to myself, "I knew if we could make it 'til daylight, we would be found."

10 *The Hunch Pays Off*

Aboard the *Sundew,* Captain Muth viewed the dawn with some relief. Finally, the lookouts aboard the searching vessels would be able to do a decent job of scanning the waters around them. What about his own hunch to search near Gull Island, would it pay off?

Captain Muth describes the event that all aboard the Sundew *had been hoping for:*

When we arrived close to Gull Island at around eight that morning, the lookout alongside me in the wheelhouse was one of our cooks, Richard Selison. He was a wonderful cook, but he was also a good seaman. He was one of the few crewmembers that wasn't seasick. I have a theory that, if a cook ever got seasick, he would never survive aboard a ship. I've served with many cooks over the years and, in general, found this observation to be true. This cook was no exception, and I was glad to have him aboard the *Sundew.*

Suddenly, he said, "Captain, I see something up ahead."

I asked, "Where?"

The cook replied, "Almost dead ahead." Upon looking through my binoculars to where the cook was pointing, I saw that he was right. I could see what appeared to be two men in a boat. They'd be visible when they came up on top of a wave and then disappear into the trough. There were definitely two people, but were they from the *Bradley*? The first thought that crossed my mind was these might be a couple of hunters from

76

High Island who had weathered the storm and were trying to get back to Charlevoix. I put that thought aside when we determined it was not a boat that the men were on but a raft. We knew then that these were probably two survivors from the *Bradley*.

Warren Toussaint recalls the excitement of finding survivors:

I remember some guy running into sickbay where I was napping and shaking me. Then he said, "The Old Man wants you on the buoy deck immediately, Doc. We have two survivors." I thought it was a dream. Survivors? I ran out on deck, and I looked to where we were going. I could see this life raft about 200 yards away.

When I saw the two guys on the raft, I called the bridge and I said, "I need some help. I'm planning to put the survivors in the chief's quarters, which will give me more room to function." Because sickbay is so small, if we put two men in there, we will hardly be able to move around. I told the captain I would need men to assist me, one on each limb to slowly massage their extremities to get some circulation back. Captain Muth said, "No problem, anything you want, just let me know."

I put about five blankets on each of the two Stokes litters, and I got them on deck right away. I had a bunch of the seamen come over, and I said, "Now, I want you to shake the blankets out so the minute we get the men on the litters you can flip the blankets on them." That way they would be covered with those good wool blankets. I didn't know what kind of condition survivors would be in.

Frank remembers the moment of rescue:

On the raft, we watched the *Sundew* approach with growing

excitement. Now, you have to keep in mind that the seas were running 20 to 25 feet high. The raft was being tossed around and so was the *Sundew*. I was really impressed with the captain's seamanship. He brought the *Sundew* parallel to the raft, quite a distance away, then let her drift in, putting us in the lee of his ship, thus calming the waves. When he came up alongside, the crew threw Elmer and me a line, which we tried to grab but couldn't. We hadn't realized that, in our weakened condition, we couldn't even lift our arms.

Captain Muth recalls the scene from his perspective on the bridge of the Sundew:

When we came up to the raft, the ship was still rolling quite a bit. The crew on the buoy deck draped the cargo net over the side. All of the deck force were wearing lifejackets and those that would attempt the rescue had ropes tied around their waists. Two of the crew, probably boatswain's mates or leading seamen, leapt down into the raft. Even though they were quite agile at jumping on buoys, this was a hairy operation in the heavy seas. When the ship rolled in the direction of the raft it would rise to almost level with the *Sundew's* deck. When the ship rolled the opposite direction, the raft would drop as much as 10 or 15 feet.

Robert Fitz and two others began to crawl down the cargo net. Fitz remembers thinking:

"This is dangerous. We could get pinned between the raft and the ship." The cargo net hung near the point where the *Sundew's* sides curved under. I feared that if the ship quickly rolled towards the raft, one of us could be crushed between the two. It was dangerous; there's no doubt about it."

Captain Muth picks up the story:

As the ship rolled to port and the raft came up, one of

78

the boatswain's mates, a wiry Italian-American from Iron Mountain, passed those two survivors up to the men on the cargo net, who, in turn, handed them up to the men on the deck. This took quite a bit of muscle and an equal amount of know-how. I was pleased with the performance of the crew, and I think our people back in Cleveland at the district office were satisfied with what we did with the number of people we had on board.

The two survivors were very stiff and very cold. Robert Fitz recalls how he felt as he helped bring Frank & Elmer aboard:

I was just happy for them, happy as could be. Elmer appeared to me to be an older person; I was just 26 at the time. I remember thinking, "What are you doing out here on a job like this at your age?" Really, he was only 43, but he appeared so old. Their faces were ashen and their lips were a ghastly blue. Their hair and eyebrows were encased with ice, as was every piece of their clothing. They weren't entirely aware of what was going on as they were taken away. They knew they were being rescued and everything, but they were not able to communicate very well with us. It was just too darn cold.

I recall my sheer astonishment (no exaggeration) at how they survived all that time under those conditions. I remember trying to put myself in their position, and I concluded without a doubt, that I couldn't have made it. I felt that they must have had a tremendous will to live.

When we got the survivors on the deck, we put a man on each arm and leg and carried them to the stretchers. When they were secure, we quickly took them to the chief's quarters, giving them over to the corpsman. Back on deck, we turned our attention to the raft, which was ice covered and very slippery. We were able to bring it aboard using the boom. We placed the raft on the buoy deck and secured it.

The raft being taken aboard the *Sundew*
Photo Credit--AP Wire

Captain Muth recalls how his crew cared for the survivors:

They had to carry the men in a wide straddle position. At one point, they had one man on each leg and one on each arm, carrying the survivors across the deck. The ship was rolling quite heavily, and the decks were wet, so this was necessary to maintain balance rather than taking a chance on dropping or injuring whom we later came to know as Mr. Fleming and Mr. Mays. Handling them with care, they were placed on the stretchers and taken to the Chief Petty Officer's quarters. I placed them in the care of Warren Toussaint, my hospital corpsman. I told Toussaint, "When you feel that they are able to talk, let me know, and I will come down and interview them."

Toussaint describes Frank and Elmer's condition:

Crewmen carry Frank Mays across the *Sundew's* pitching deck
Photo Credit--Detroit Free Press

My first job was to treat them. They looked like they were in bad shape, with their faces all swollen. They were in a kind of daze at first. They had that blank look, like they're asking, "Am I really saved?"

In my preliminary evaluation, I took their temperature, and they were normal, which fascinated me. Amazingly, they were not in bad shape. They were both healthy guys. The only thing I worried about was that they might come down with pneumonia because of being out in that kind of weather for 15 hours. Being thrown in the water several times couldn't have done them much good either.

I removed their wet clothes and put men to work kneading their legs to get the circulation flowing. They started coming around, so I let the Captain know that they were ready to be interviewed.

Captain Muth recalls the first time he met Frank and Elmer:

I guess it was about ten minutes or so when Warren called up and said, "They're awake and alert. They are ready to talk." He also indicated to me that they were probably well enough to stay out if we wanted to continue the search.

Statement of Elmer H. Fleming, First Mate
of the Steamer Carl Bradley

"I returned from evening meal to resume pilot watch at approximately 1720, 18 November 1958, and along about 1740 heard a "thud", looked aft and saw after end already settling in the water. The Captain was on the bridge and sounded the alarm bells and blew whistle (emergency or abandon ship). I went to telephone and came in on 51 to give Mayday, giving our position and saying we were going to break in two and sink at any minute. Recieved reply from WLC Rogers City also called CG then the line broke before any reply was recieved. "ropped telephone and returned to room for life jacket. When I returned from my room to the bridge front half of the ship was going under. Climbed over rail on port side to check and see if life raft was free. In the meantime ship listed to port so every one climbed to the high side (starboard). Fell overboard and life raft followed. When I came up I grabbed for the lifeboat and held on. I wasn't 20 feet away when stern disappeared straight down followed by an explosion. Frank Mays was on life raft when I grabbed for it. Gary Strzelecki and Dennis Meredith swam to the life raft and Frank and I helped them aboard. The life raft flipped almost immediatly all 4 men got back on raft. Put out sea anchors, rode along until about 2230 when we flipped again. All got on again except Dennis Meredith. He could not get on the raft. We tried to get him on but couldn't so held on to him for about three (3) hours. Unable to help Meredith and he went under. Lost sea anchore. Told men not to sleep but to keep awake and keep talking. Gary seemed to go to sleep and we tried to get him awake, he wanted to go swimming. We fought to keep him aboard but he finally went overboard about daybreak. At the time of breaking up we were about 6 miles off Boulder Reef Buoy and about 1 mile northward, 16.5 miles off South Fox Island northend.

Witness by: H. D. MUTH
LCDR, USCG
Commanding Officer
USCGC SUNDEW (WAGL 404)

Elmer H. Fleming

Statement of Frank Louis Mays AB
of the Steamer Carl Bradley

I was in conveyor room at time of crash. Ran topside. Heard someone say ship was breaking in two. Went to room for lifejacket, took one look astern and saw center go up 60 feet in air. Told other crew members in vicinity "up to life raft". Got in life raft and checked oars untied one end of them. Was still in raft when it went over the side. Came up about 4 feet from raft, swam to it and climbed aboard. We (Mr. Fleming and I) hollered to crew members but they couldn't get to raft. From this point on story is as told by Mr. Fleming.

Frank L. Mays

Witnessed by: H. D. MUTH
LCDR, USCG
Commanding Officer
USCGC SUNDEW (WAGL 404)

The statement Frank & Elmer made 10 minutes after being rescued

I went down to the Chief Petty Officer's quarters and asked them how they felt. Both of them said that they felt pretty good. I asked them if they had any explanation as to why the *Bradley* sank. Each responded with his own idea. I asked them about their experiences during the night. Elmer did most of the talking and said that there had been two other men on the raft beside themselves. He told me about Dennis, and then, about how Gary had left the raft voluntarily and tried to swim for it. I asked them whether they wanted us to take them back to Charlevoix at that time, or did they want us to remain in the area and continue to search? They both were emphatic that they were all right and that they wanted us to stay out and look for their shipmates. Before I left, I told them that if at any time they felt that they wanted to get back to port, I would immediately break off the search and head for Charlevoix. Their reply was, "No. We would appreciate it if you would continue to search and see if you can find any more survivors."

When I finished interviewing the survivors, I returned to the bridge. As the on-site commander of the search effort, I would have to turn the job over to the captain of the *Hollyhock* should I need to return to port. I called the corpsman and told him, if at any point in time he felt that we should get Mr. Mays and Mr. Fleming back to port and into a hospital, that he was to inform me immediately.

A short time later, I received a report from the *Hollyhock* that the aircraft had sighted an overturned lifeboat about one mile south of the raft's position. When we arrived at the lifeboat, we saw that it had no occupants, so we decided to take it aboard. Just then, we received word from the *Hollyhock* that they were encountering bodies in the water up at the northern tip of Gull Island.

Jack Coppens aboard the *Sundew's* ramp boat
with bodies from the *Bradley's* crew
Photo Credit--Life Magazine, December 1958

I decided to abandon the lifeboat and join the *Hollyhock*. The cargo net was put over the side of the buoy deck again, and two men were detailed to try to retrieve the bodies as the *Sundew* came up to them. Occasionally, they needed to use a boat hook to get the victims close enough to bring aboard.

Robert Fitz helped retrieve the unfortunate sailors. He remembers:

I helped pick up a number of bodies, and it really was sad. One of the men we found must have worked in the engine room, because he was wearing a gray shirt, like the type that would be worn there. I know one worked in the galley, because he was wearing his lifejacket over a white T-shirt and thin, white cotton pants. We also recovered one good sized person. We put them on the buoy deck by the raft. In the heavy seas, it was difficult to chase all the bodies down with the *Sundew,* so the captain put our boats over the side to recover them.

Warrant Boatswain Jack Coppens took charge of the Sundew's ramp boat (so known because it had a forward ramp like a landing craft), and set off to recover more bodies.

We spent maybe an hour and a half searching for bodies. The spray was so bad that it was like being in a snowstorm, only a lot wetter. There were airplanes on the scene, but we couldn't talk to them. When a plane would spot a body, they'd wiggle their wings and circle to show us where to look. We'd motor over to the area, pull alongside a body, wait until a wave brought it up, and grab it. With the heavy gray lifejackets they were wearing, it took all three of us to pull each poor soul aboard. I think we had five bodies in our boat.

When we returned to the *Sundew,* we had a heck of a time getting the boat back aboard. The ship was still rolling, and the falls got all tangled while we were trying to haul the boat up. In the five to ten minutes it took to get things straightened out, we got slammed against the *Sundew* so bad that one side of the ramp boat was bashed in.

Warren Toussaint remembers they were able to recover eight men that day:

Each time a victim was brought on board, I was called up from the sickbay to evaluate him. I hoped that I would find another survivor with a breath of life in him, but they were all deceased. We placed the belongings of these unfortunate souls in large envelopes with their names on them. I particularly remember one of the victims, a cook who had sailed the lakes for 30 years. This was to be his last trip and in his pocket was $1500.

During all of this, I had been in regular contact with Dr. Lawrence Grate in Charlevoix, and kept him informed of Frank and Elmer's condition. Both were fully aware of their surroundings the whole time I was dealing with them. They didn't sleep very much, but that isn't unusual because their adrenaline was going at such a rate. They were so glad to be alive.

One thing Frank and Elmer did ask for was food, and I wouldn't give them any because that was my training. I said, "No, and I will tell you why. If you eat now, you will probably throw up." I told them, "I'll get you something, just give me time. We'll wait a couple of hours, and if you're still all right and awake, I'll give you some coffee or cocoa."

We finally did give them some cocoa, but we had trouble even doing that because every single particle of food on our ship was destroyed. We had rolled so hard in the storm that the great big cans of stuff like corn and beans had all been burst open. The entire galley was covered in ruined food. Add in the pots, pans and knives that were thrown around, and it looked as if someone had tossed a hand grenade in there. They locked the door and nobody could go in. The paint locker in the bow was in the same condition. Over 100 cans were split open. Because of the fumes and the danger of fire, nobody was allowed in that room either.

11 *They've Found Survivors!*

At about 9:15 AM, word that two survivors had been found hit Rogers City. The survivor's names had not been released, so there was hope in every waiting home that their loved ones had been spared. The families held their collective breath as they waited for the phone to ring with the news that would change their lives forever.

The news media had inundated Rogers City, which was both a blessing and a curse. It was a blessing inasmuch as the families devoured whatever was printed in the papers and listened nonstop to the radio and television, hoping for any new information. It was a curse in that some media individuals tried to exploit the families to sensationalize their stories.

Janette Brege recalls her impression of the pushy press and how they treated Frank Mays's wife right after the news of Frank's survival had been released.

Right after I heard Frank's and Elmer's names over the air, I noticed the media coming down our street. I lived right across the street from Frank and Marlys and saw several cars pull up in front of their house. I immediately went over to see if I could do anything to help Marlys.

When I got there, I saw that Marlys had her mother and a few friends there to help her. I watched aghast as a reporter picked Frank Jr. out of his crib, stuck him in his mother's arms and started snapping pictures. I think Marlys was kind of in a state of shock at that time. I noticed that they had some kind of device attached to the telephone. I asked

88

them about it, and they said that they were sending pictures through on the telephone line. That was my first encounter with the press, seeing how they just took right over. There was no doubt in my mind that the press knew people were in shock, and they were taking advantage of it. Of course, this was headline news.

Representatives of the Bradley Company arrived to take Marlys to Charlevoix. While fixing her hair and smoothing her dress she regained her composure enough to answer a few more questions. When asked how she felt about Frank's rescue, she replied, "I'm happy, very happy, but I'm sorry that so many others wives are sad. Frank will be 27 on Monday

Frank's wife, Marlys, with sons Michael and Mark
Photo Credit--Presque Isle County Advance

and we're going to have a big birthday, Thanksgiving and Christmas party all rolled into one."

Her son Michael had been outside playing. Before Marlys left the house she called him in and posed for a photograph with him and her son Mark.

12 *Wednesday Afternoon Return to Charlevoix*

Throughout the long night and morning, Captain Muth had led the search for the Bradley's crew from the Sundew's bridge. Hours had passed since the survivors were brought aboard, and it was time to make a decision:

I had been monitoring the progress of the survivors all morning, when around noon, I received a report from the hospital corpsman that made me decide it was time to suspend our search and return to port. The corpsman advised me that although Fleming and Mays were still desirous of our remaining on the scene and searching, it would be better if they were taken to a hospital. He had noticed their temperatures rising, which is the first sign of pneumonia. With the best interests of the survivors in mind, I asked the *Hollyhock* to remain on the scene and headed back to Charlevoix.

* * *

Shortly after Captain Muth turned over on-scene command of the search to the *Hollyhock*, a message came over the radio from the merchant vessel *M/V Transontario*. At 13:14, from a position close to the west shore of High Island, the *Transontario* had taken aboard a man that still had a spark of life in him.

This created a scurry of activity, and preparations were made to bring medical help out to the *Transontario*. One of the searching helicopters was directed by the Coast Guard Base at Traverse City to head to Beaver Island to pick up a doctor. Frank E. Luton, a 79 year-old, retired physician, had volunteered for the dangerous undertaking. The only doctor on Beaver Island, he was willing to risk his life to save that of the dying sailor. Doctor Luton would not let mere age stand in the way of what he saw to be his duty.

The plan was to take Dr. Luton out by helicopter to the *Transontario* and lower him by hoist to the deck of the ship. In the high winds and heavy seas, this would be a very risky maneuver, even for a much younger man.

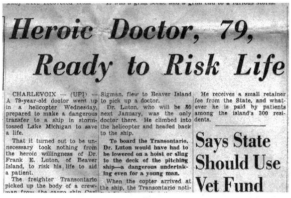

Detroit Free Press, November 20, 1958

When Captain Muth heard this, he went down and told Elmer and Frank that another survivor had been found. Frank asked, "Did he have a beard? What was he wearing?" Captain Muth described what he had heard of the man's appearance and instantly they knew that Gary Strzelecki had been found. Frank and Elmer began praying for their shipmate, as they waited for more news.

Meanwhile, the helicopter had just arrived at the *Transontario,* and Dr. Luton was getting prepared, when they received the heart breaking news that Gary had passed away. Doctor Luton's heroic efforts were much appreciated, but his services would no longer be needed. The helicopter turned around and flew him back to Beaver Island.

Warren Toussaint remembers the Sundew's return to port:

We arrived at Charlevoix about 4:30 in the evening, just about dusk. We were just about to enter the channel when I said to the captain, "You know we have eight bodies out on the buoy deck and were going into port." I knew people along the channel and on the bridge would be higher than the ship and able to look down on her decks. The waiting crowd was sure to contain some family members and I didn't want them to see their loved ones in this way. I suggested to the captain, " Why don't we take a big tarp and cover them up so nobody would know they were there?" Captain Muth agreed and a tarp was placed over the unfortunate souls.

The *Sundew* made its way up the channel and then through the highway bridge, which was lined with people. But instead of tying up at their regular mooring, the captain made a circle on Round Lake and tied up at the city pier where the ferryboats docked. He could see all the people and cars were lined up there.

It was a somber place to be that day. Usually, when we would return to port, people would smile and wave. This time, we were greeted with total silence. The only sound was the buzz of news media aircraft circling overhead. As we tied up, I could see a huge number of expectant, waiting faces. I could also see waiting ambulances and hearses.

After we tied up, we waited for the authorities to come on board. The medical officer for the county of Charlevoix, Dr. Grate, went first to check on the condition of Mr. Mays and Mr. Fleming. He came out saying that, for all they had been through, they were in remarkable shape.

A crowd waits at City Pier for the *Sundew*
Photo Credit--Detroit Times

13 *Back in the Land of the Living*

Frank remembers the examination:

While the hospital corpsman told him of the measures he took to treat us, Dr. Grate checked us over real well. The doctor commended Toussaint on his actions, then the two of them put their heads together to decide how to proceed. I think they decided it would be in Elmer's and my best interest if they put ashore all those that did not survive before we saw them. But apparently, it didn't work out that way. Lying on the stretcher just before they took us out the door, I remember Dr. Grate saying, "Close your eyes, you guys, so you don't look at all these people that showed up." I didn't close my eyes. They brought me out of the room, and we made a right turn and then went up the ramp. As we crossed the *Sundew*'s deck, I looked over and saw several bodies underneath a tarp.

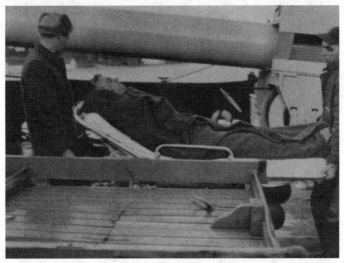

Robert Fitz(R) helps carry Elmer Fleming off the *Sundew*
Photo Credit--Life Magazine

95

They quickly took us up the ramp to the dock. The City Pier ran parallel to the street with a large parking lot that provided easy access for those loading and unloading ships. When they carried me down the ramp, I was amazed how many cars were lined up along the shore. The crowd was huge but mostly silent. The spectators cleared about a 20-foot path, making it easier for the Coast Guard crewmembers to carry me to the ambulance. Elmer was carried off right behind me.

As I was carried through crowd, I was stunned at the range of expressions I could see on the faces of those that had gathered along the route. There were the curious ones who came to see what the commotion was. There were wives, children, and parents of the *Sundew's* crew that were relieved

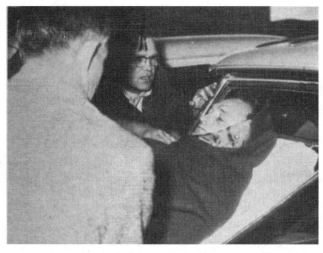

Frank Mays is loaded into a waiting ambulance
Photo Credit--Detroit Times

as they watched their men working on the deck. There were those who stared in wonderment, questioning how we could have survived last night. Then there were the familiar faces of some of the family members of the *Bradley's* crew. I think they were happy that I had survived but afraid that their loved one might be one of the bodies under the tarp, or worse yet, still missing on the lake. Jostling their way through the crowd were the reporters, trying to ask questions, and cameramen, snapping pictures as quick as they could.

Just before Dr. Grate shut the door of the ambulance, he said that he would meet me at the hospital. As the door was closing, the curious sneaked a last peek and then I was taken away.

We arrived at the Charlevoix Hospital minutes later, where some male orderlies met me at the door and put me in a double room with Elmer. Since we were just wrapped in blankets and didn't have any clothes on, they carefully dressed us in hospital gowns and placed us in bed with hot water bottles surrounding our bodies. Dr. Grate had come in sometime during this process, and when the orderlies were done, he checked our vital signs again. He told us that, although our hands and faces were red and very swollen, neither Elmer nor I had frostbite. He had expected much worse because the reports stated that the air and water temperatures the night before had been around 40 degrees with 65 MPH winds, producing an incredible wind chill. I was surprised but grateful that I never had a problem with frostbite.

His examination finished, Dr. Grate asked, "Do you boys drink?"

Both Elmer and I replied, "Sure!"

He then called directions to his staff, "Get these boys a drink."

He gave us each a shot of whiskey. I guess he wanted to get us warmed up inside.

The staff treated us well, but they wouldn't let us do anything on our own. Dr. Grate told us "You have to bathe every day, but you're not going to be by yourself. Two guys are going to go in there with you."

Dr. Grate left, and within a few minutes our wives were brought in. Upon seeing them, our spirits soared. Their radiant smiles were contagious, and soon we were all grinning. From the relief in their faces, I could see that they had been through their own ordeal, and we shared a quiet moment of thankfulness that things had ended the way they did. A few minutes later, Mary and Elmer were joined by their 15 year old son, Douglas.

Around seven that evening, our male orderlies wheeled our beds down the hall to the solarium. During the day, this room was filled with bright sunlight entering through large windows that overlooked Lake Michigan. The room was normally used by patients who would come to sit and talk

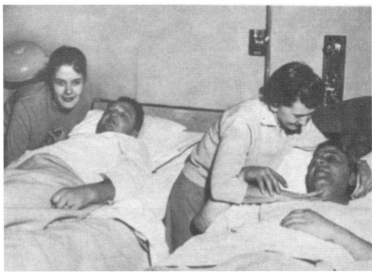

Frank and Elmer are reunited with their wives at Charlevoix Hospital
Photo Credit--Stag Magazine

Detroit Free Press, November 20, 1958

with visitors or who just wanted to find a quiet place to relax and enjoy the view. This night, the room took on a totally different function. As we were wheeled to the front of the room, I was confronted by a sea of anxious faces, all eager for news. The room was packed wall-to-wall with media personnel. There were newspaper reporters, magazine writers, photographers and TV cameramen, all waiting to hear what we had to say. While I waited for the news conference to start, I remember looking out through the large windows and seeing the white-capped waves of a still angry Lake Michigan slamming against the shore.

My reverie was interrupted when a sudden barrage of flashbulbs lit the room as the reporters began to take pictures of Elmer and I. With our wives smiling by our sides, we did the best we could to put on a good face for the cameras. Then Dr. Grate announced that, since we had been through a lot of stress and physical exhaustion, he would allow only a short interview. As the doctor talked, I looked over at Elmer; his red face was windburned and quite puffy. I felt my own face and wondered how long it would be before the swelling would go down. Even so, Elmer had a smile on his face. You could tell he was glad to be alive. Elmer hadn't had any quality sleep for nearly 30 hours and yet, you could see that he still had his confidence and his wits about him. Being the senior officer, most of the questions were directed to him. We both spoke during the interview, but Elmer did most of the talking.

The first question Elmer was asked was, "Where were you when the disaster struck?"

Elmer replied, "I was at my station in the pilothouse when I heard a heavy thud from somewhere in the ship and an alarm began to clang. I spun around and looked back aft down the deck, where I saw the stern of the boat was sagging. I knew right then that we were going to sink." He told the assembled reporters about the "Mayday" message he sent. Elmer seemed proud as he stated, "It turned out, that the Coast Guard heard me up and down the lake."

Fleming went on, "I had no lifejacket, and about that time, a fellow brought me a ring buoy. I didn't want a ring buoy, and I stepped out on the main deck, where I saw we were awash already." He then went on to tell about how he went down to his quarters, got a lifejacket, and came back up and stood by the raft. Elmer continued to tell his story to the hushed audience, "There was a raft right on deck next to where I was standing, so I went over to see if it was going to float. I stepped into water and picked up one end of the raft. The heavy superstructure started to turn the ship sideways, and when she started to roll, she really went. I was thrown into the water, and the raft came up behind me. I came up about a foot from the raft and grabbed it. We climbed on the raft and held on with all we had," Elmer continued, "I could see some of the other men climbing to the high side of the superstructure as it was rolling over. That's actually good seamanship, but it didn't work out for them."

They asked me the same questions. I told them how I ended up in the water, then told them how Elmer and I were able to help bring two other men aboard.

I finished speaking and Elmer added, "Mays and I were climbing on the raft, and we could hear those fellows hollering, and we were doing some hollering ourselves. One of our workboats was in the water, but it was all crushed up. There were men in the water, but the waves were so high you couldn't see them." He added, "I hung on and couldn't see anybody else, though we had ring buoys with water lights on them. We couldn't see because of the huge waves. We could only hear them hollering."

Elmer repeated what I had said about helping the two guys onto the raft. Then, he told them about the sinking of the aft section. He said, "While I was watching, about 250 feet of the stern section went right straight down - fast." He finished off his answer by telling them that after the stern went down, we didn't hear any more hollering.

When the reporters asked us what happened to the other two men who where on the raft with us, Elmer's whole demeanor changed. He stared down and swallowed hard. "We lost them during the night," he said. "The raft flipped completely over near midnight, and only one came back then." I could see the turmoil inside Elmer as he spoke.

We had talked earlier and decided that this was not the time to tell the whole truth about Dennis and Gary. We wanted to tell their families what had happened before anyone else. We also knew we had to keep Dennis Meredith's and Gary Strzelecki's identities a secret until their families could be properly notified. Looking at Elmer, I could see the emotion was getting to him. He had tried so hard to take care of those boys. He was like a father figure to them, and he felt so bad about their loss. Throughout that long night on the raft, he had encouraged them and tried to keep them from going to sleep. He had even used his own body to try to shelter Dennis from the spray.

101

When I saw that Elmer wasn't going to be able to speak, I knew I had to do something. Speaking up, I told the reporters, "The raft flipped over three or four times during the night. After the last flip, Fleming and I were the only persons to make it back, and we were alone the rest of the time." I quickly changed the subject. "I was never so cold in my life."

Recovering somewhat, Elmer joined in, "I didn't notice the cold at first," he said, "But later, I got so numb I was afraid I couldn't hang on to the raft with my hands." As he spoke his voice became stronger, "I swallowed a lot of water, but I always managed to get a good grip on the raft when I got back to it."

As the interview wore on, they asked about the *Christian Sartori*. I told them that we only had occasional glimpses of them, adding, "Those men really had nerve." Elmer joined in, "The men on those boats are to be congratulated. They were rolling about 50 °. It took great seamanship and courage to work out there."

I spoke up, "There was never any doubt in my mind that someone would find us if we could last through the night." I continued, "I prayed a lot, and I got pretty scared when I found that there was ice forming on my hair and crusted on my jacket, but I still felt that if we could make it 'til daylight we'd be okay."

Elmer added, "The other boats knew where we were. We knew that." I concluded with the statement, "When it got to be daylight, I was sure our prayers would be answered."

At that point, Doctor Grate spoke up, commenting that, although we were suffering from shock and exposure, he felt we were in pretty good condition. He then said, "It's an amazing piece of human endurance." He then told the reporters that after all Elmer and I had been through, we needed our rest; therefore, he was ending the interview.

The reporters turned their attention to our wives. Asked how she felt about her husband's rescue, Mary Fleming said, "I'm happy my husband is safe, but I can't be completely happy because so many others are dead or still missing." She then told the reporters she never lost hope that Elmer would survive. She said, "I knew how strict Elmer and the captain were about lifeboat drills. I know if courage and seamanship would do it, my husband would survive."

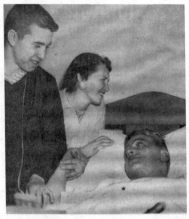

Elmer Fleming's son Doug visits him
Photo Credit--Presque Isle County Advance

Mary and their son, Doug accompanied Elmer as he was pushed on his bed back to our room. My orderly was about to follow when one of the reporters asked my wife about how she had handled last night. My wife Marlys replied, "I've been praying ever since I heard that the boat had gone down. When I heard that there were only two survivors, I realized the odds were against me, but I never stopped hoping." Then she grabbed my hand and smiled.

As my orderly began to push me toward my room, I realized how exhausted I was. It had been over 30 hours since I'd had any real rest and I was starting to feel it. Not long after I reached my room, I fell into a deep sleep.

Back at the pier, Captain Muth was being questioned by the press while cameramen shot footage and snapped pictures of the scene. He talked to the news media that were at the dock regarding the search efforts, what the results were, what he had encountered, and so forth. When he was asked what the men said when they were taken from the raft, Captain Muth replied, "Well, they were very happy to see us." When they questioned him on how Fleming and Mays had survived that night, he replied, "They had a little help. Someone looked after them."

Captain Harold Muth answers questions for the press
Photo credit--Detroit Times

Working along with local officials, Captain Muth supervised the removal of the eight victims aboard the *Sundew* to a temporary morgue set up in the Charlevoix City Hall. That grim duty accomplished, Captain Muth recalls, " After not having had any sleep for a couple of days, I was pretty tired, so I went to bed at about 10:00 PM."

When the *Hollyhock* joined the *Sundew* in Charlevoix later that day, she added another nine bodies to the grim total. Gary Strzelecki's body was still on the *Transontario*, and arrangements were being made to have it be flown back to Rogers City from Milwaukee.

Back at the dock, Chief Warrant Boatswain James Cropper of the *Hollyhock* had his own tale to tell. When asked how the lake was that night, he replied,

> "It was the roughest sea I ever saw, and I've seen a
> few. At times, the pitching and the rolling and the
> valleys were so deep, it looked like all the water
> had disappeared and was going uphill in front of
> us. The ocean sailors kid us lake men about our
> little ponds. I'd better never hear that again. Last
> night was a visit to Hell." *The Detroit Times, Thursday,*
> *November 20, 1958*

Norman Hoeft, manager of the Bradley Transportation Company, came from Rogers City to meet the *Sundew* and arrange for transfer of the survivors to the hospital. Now, he helped other company officials make tentative identifications of the bodies. The names of the dead were relayed back to Rogers City, where officials began the heartbreaking task of notifying the families of their loss.

In Rogers City, word quickly got out that Lewis Patterson, manager of the northern district for Michigan Limestone, and George R. Jones, District Superintendent for Industrial Relations, were performing the unpleasant task of breaking the grim news to the families. Lights burned all night long as the emotionally exhausted families waited in fear of a knock at the door.

One by one, 18 families learned the awful news. For the others, there was nothing to do but wait, hope and pray.

A Coast Guard 40-foot lifeboat from Charlevoix
joins the search on November, 19th
Photo Credit--Detroit Free Press

14 Hope Dwindling, the Search Continues

Early Thursday morning (November 20th), the *Sundew* and *Hollyhock* planned an early departure, hoping to get to the search site by sunrise. As day began to break, the air search resumed, with a USCG Gruman Albatross, callsign UF 1273, departing Traverse City at around 7:30 AM. Other government and private planes also began to arrive to assist with the search.

Coast Guard helicopters join in the search
Photo Credit--ML Screenings

While this was going on, the Grand Traverse County Sheriff's Department had enlisted the aid of local volunteers and was making plans for a ground search. Two hours later, three helicopters carrying searchers left Traverse City and headed for the islands within the search area. The *Sundew* and the *Hollyhock* put shore parties on High Island and Gull Island to assist in the effort. Searchers on Gull Island discovered one lifejacket and a considerable amount of debris on the southwest shore. On the south shore of High Island, several lifejackets were discovered, along with the capsized lifeboat that the *Sundew* saw on Wednesday morning. Land searches on Squaw, Garden, Trout, Beaver, and Whisky Islands did not reveal any wreckage, with the exception of some debris found in the water off Whiskey Island. There were no other signs of survivors, and no other bodies recovered. In all, some 150 people helped in the land search of the islands in the vicinity of the sinking. During the search, winds speeds were clocked at 40 MPH and the temperature was about 40 degrees. With the wind chill factor so low, searchers believed there was little chance of finding anyone alive.

> "It's pretty remote that anybody is alive out there, but we just can't give up until we have done a thorough job of searching," said Chief Boatswain Joseph Etienne, Coast Guard group commander at Charlevoix. *(Detroit Free Press, Friday, November 21, 1958)*

In Chicago, as the *Christian Sartori* docked, newspaper reporters were waiting to interview Captain Paul Mueller. The *Sartori's* skipper was one of the last men to see the *Bradley* afloat, and the media longed to hear his story. Below are portions of his interview that appeared in newspapers that day.

> The second mate and I were on the bridge when flames suddenly shot up from the *Bradley's* afterdeck," Mueller said.

> "A blast followed, hiding the ship in a dark cloud. Three minutes later, the cloud was gone and so was the ship."

Mueller, a wartime German U-boat officer, said his ship was only four miles from the *Bradley* at that time. He immediately gave the orders to head for the scene of the wreck.

"In that storm, it took us two hours to reach the spot where the *Bradley* went down," Mueller said. He said ordinarily it would have taken only 15 minutes.

"In six years of sailing the Great Lakes, I have never seen such rough waters as on this last trip," the captain said.

"By the time we got to the scene, it was already dark," he added.

He reported all he found was a smashed tank and a raincoat....

Crewmen on the *Sartori* spotted red flares on the horizon shortly after the *Bradley* sank. Mueller said they were probably from survivors. "They must have used up their flares quickly because they saw us nearby, but the storm made it impossible for us to reach them in time." The *Sartori* hunted for survivors in the area for ten hours, Mueller said, while a 60 MPH wind whipped 30 foot high waves against the German ship.

Bay City Times - November 21st, 1958

Captain Mueller also said, "We on this ship are very happy to hear that some of the men have been rescued. It was not a pleasant feeling for us to find nothing but that floating tank. We thought for a long time that all hands must have been lost in such weather. We saw no lifeboats and it seemed impossible for a swimmer to survive. We searched anyway. We wish we could have done more."

Detroit Times - November 19, 1958

Meanwhile, the German freighter, *Transontario* had arrived in Milwaukee, and Captain Walter Zeplien had made

The captain and crew of the *Transontario* stand at attention as Gary Strzelecki's body is taken ashore

Photo Credit--Bay City Times

arrangements to release Gary Strzelecki's body so it could be flown back to Rogers City. Meeting him at the dock were Gary's uncle Frank Strzelecki and E. A. Kehr of the Michigan Limestone Division of the U.S. Steel Corporation. In a show of respect, Captain Zeplien and his crew stood at attention as the flag draped body was brought ashore.

When the German Captain was interviewed at the dock, he was quoted as saying he wished that there had been more that he and his crew could of done. The captain and crew of the *Transontario* were typical of the mariners that had responded to the *Bradley's* "Mayday" call. All had acted according to the finest traditions of the sea.

* * *

The Sinking of the *Bradley* became a Nationwide news event. A mass influx of media personnel began to invade the small town of Rogers City and nearby Alpena. The small airport in Alpena wasn't prepared to handle such a large number of private planes. Robert Welch, operator of the Alpena Flying Service, noticed that traffic at the airport was busier than he had ever seen before. He said, "Our parking ramp is filled right up—we haven't got an open place on it. We have over $2,000,000 worth of airplanes on the ramp right now."

The Alpena News, Thursday 20, 1958

In addition to the large number of media personnel flying in, top officials of the United States Steel Corporation were also landing in Alpena enroute to Rogers City.

Roger Blough, chairman of the Board for United States Steel, flew from New York into Alpena and was driven up to Rogers City, arriving at 3:30 in the afternoon. He then met

111

with Chris F. Beukema, President of Michigan Limestone, who had arrived Wednesday morning. Clifford F. Hood, President of United States Steel Corporation, would arrive later that night. They had come to Rogers City to be of whatever assistance they could be in their official capacities as heads of the United States Steel Corporation.

Vice Admiral, Alfred C. Richmond, Commandant of the U.S. Coast Guard, ordered an investigation into the sinking of the *Carl D. Bradley*. He put together a Board of Inquiry to direct the investigation. Heading the board was Rear Admiral Joseph A. Kerrins, commander of the Ninth Coast Guard District. Working with Admiral Kerrins was Commander Charles E. Leising, Jr., Lieutenant Commander George H. Read, and Commander Joseph Change.

* * *

In Rogers City that Thursday morning, what little hope there was left of finding survivors quickly faded as the townspeople began to read the names of the dead in the newspaper. Of the 33 men lost on the *Bradley*, 23 were from Rogers City. Fifteen of the 18 bodies recovered would be brought to Rogers City area for burial, while the bodies of Carl Bartell, Richard Book, and John Zoho were returned to their hometowns of Kalkaska, Michigan, Portsmouth, Iowa, and Claireton, Pennsylvania.

As the bodies of the lost *Bradley* crewmen began to arrive in Rogers City, the task fell to Mayor Ken Vogelheim and local funeral directors and clergy to attempt to coordinate the scheduling of all the different memorial services.

For Father Adalbert Narloch, the Catholic priest from St. Ignatius's, it seemed an overwhelming task. Eleven of the deceased were from his parish. He began to prepare for a

112

mass funeral, knowing that over 1,000 people would come to pay their final respects. Robert E. Weller, Pastor of St. John's Lutheran Church in Rogers City, as well Pastor C. F. Boerger and Elder Ernest Burt of nearby Onaway were also preparing their churches for funeral services.

Messages of sympathy came from all over the United States. In the Detroit Free Press that day was an editorial called, "Michigan Mourns Her Sailor Sons." In the closing lines of the article it stated:

> The reason for destruction of the *Bradley* and the loss of her men can be explained only as another of Providence's inscrutable mysteries.

> We express, we are sure, the sentiments of all Michigan when we extend to the people of Rogers City our deepest sympathy in this bleak and trying hour. *The Detroit Free Press, Thursday, November 20, 1958*

As night set in, the *Sundew* and *Hollyhock* returned to Charlevoix, and the aircraft headed back to Traverse City. The search would resume at first light, Friday, November 21st.

Life preservers from the *Bradley* recovered by Coast Guardsmen
Photo Credit--The Alpena News

113

15 *Friday*

The early morning darkness of November 21st found the crew of the *Sundew* headed out for another long day of searching for the *Bradley's* crew. Joined by search planes, they sailed back and forth in a grid pattern, hoping to find some traces of the 15 men that were still missing. These search efforts were hampered by the strong winds that still prevailed, which also made it difficult for helicopters to ferry land patrols to the islands. The two 40-foot rescue boats from Charlevoix and Beaver Island also assisted in the search, but found nothing of significance. Hope had been briefly rekindled when reports of wreckage near Beaver Island had come in, but an inspection of the area had yielded no results.

That same morning, the Coast Guard convened its official inquiry at the Presque Isle County Courthouse in Rogers City. It was held in the courtroom on the second floor, and even though this session was open to the public, there were no spectators. This first session was intended to establish procedures and begin exploring the facts related to the *Bradley's* sinking. Admiral Kerrins opened the inquiry by declaring, "We are here to determine the cause of the accident and responsibility." The admiral continued, "Our hope is to prevent a recurrence."

The first item on the agenda was to establish the particulars of the *Carl D. Bradley*. The first witness called before the board was Norman O. Hoeft, general manager of the

Bradley Transportation Company. He submitted a number of documents, including the ship's Inspection Certificates from the Coast Guard and a Lloyd's of London "load-line survey" certificate. Norman Hoeft described, in full detail, the *Bradley's* engines, engine room, the cargo hold, and hatch covers, including the hatch closing devices.

At the close of the session, Admiral Kerrins indicated that the inquiry would reconvene the next day in Charlevoix, where they would interview the survivors and some of the Coast Guard personnel involved with the rescue effort.

* * *

That same day, the Rogers City High School gymnasium was being prepared for a community memorial service. A large floral anchor stood between two huge American flags in the center of the stage. This six foot white anchor, a memorial gift from the city council of Rogers City, was covered with red roses and inscribed, "Farewell, Shipmates." The large room was a flurry of activity as preparations for the day's solemn affair were underway. Fifteen caskets were neatly spaced around the floor and provisions were being made for the anticipated large turnout of people wishing to pay their respects.

The high school cafeteria became the unofficial press headquarters for the army of reporters, and it soon evolved into the town's information center. Reporters, townspeople, undertakers, and pallbearers gathered to help out, spelling names, solving problems, and deciding on protocol.

Relatives of the departed were continuing to arrive in Rogers City. Some who were in military service were able to come home due to the efforts of Red Cross representatives Jerome Kowalski and Frank Moody. Over 40 cases were handled by the pair, with the result that many servicemen made it home in time for the funeral services. James Price and Barry Vallee were able to come all the way from Germany.

* * *

As the people of Rogers City prepared to bury their dead, messages of sympathy were arriving from all over the country.

Many of the letters received were similar to this one from a former Rogers City resident then living in Grand Rapids. Sent to Harry H. Whiteley, editor of the Presque Isle County Advance, it sums up the need that many people felt to try to help the families of the lost sailors.

Dear Harry:

Attached is my check in the amount of $100.00 made out to the Rogers City Disaster Fund, which I hope you will organize and promote for the wives and children of the men lost in the disaster of yesterday, the sinking of the steamer *Carl D. Bradley*.

I know of no person, nor a better media, more suited to promote this idea. The service clubs of Rogers City, the American Legion, and many other citizens should give you able assistance in this cause. This calamity, with the large loss of life, would be extremely difficult for the families of these men at any time of the year, however, coming at the advent of the Holiday Season, the loss will be doubly felt by the wives and children left behind... This tragedy is a terrible one for the little town, these people left to sail the lakes. I hope others feel as I do about making this Christmas a little less tragic, at least for the Children."

Sincerely,

Herbert Trapp

Members of the news media were not immune to the tragedy and its impact on the sailor's families. Reporters from the <u>Detroit Times</u> were so touched by their plight that the company elected to give $1,000 to help establish a fund for the children made fatherless by the *Bradley's* sinking. Working with representatives from Rogers City, they established the <u>Ship Disaster Children's Fund</u> and used their newspaper to solicit donations from their readers.

The people of Rogers City had indeed been struck a terrible blow. As Eleanor Tulgetske, wife of *Bradley* wheelsman, Earl Tulgetske, put it, "I always watched the boats, and I knew the town lived by them. Now, the town is dying by them."

Detroit Free Press, Thursday, November 20, 1958

Many shared her feelings that day, yet Rogers City was far from dead. The community pulled together, and with help from others in the surrounding area, did what they could to lessen the burden of the grieving families. The Women's Civil League put out an appeal for accommodations to house the relatives and friends summoned by the tragedy, and by evening, over 50 townspeople had opened their homes to the visitors. Baby sitters were recruited to mind small children while their parents attended the various services. Others offered to drive family members to the services or to help in whatever way they could.

By nightfall on that Friday, over 6,000 grieving relatives, friends, and townspeople had come to the Rogers City High school gymnasium to pay their respects. The deceased that were Catholic were then taken to the auditorium at St. Ignatius church, and a holy hour was held from 7:30 to 8:30 PM. After the events of that long day, the townspeople went home physically and emotionally exhausted, knowing that tomorrow would be even harder to deal with.

Thousands pay their respects in the Rogers City school gymnasium
Photo Credit-Detroit Times

16 *Saturday*

As the sun rose over the hills surrounding Traverse City that Saturday morning, search planes took off for another day of searching. There was little hope of finding anyone alive, but they still had to try. Meanwhile, the *Sundew* and *Hollyhock* remained moored to the dock in Charlevoix, so their crews could be available to answer questions from the officers investigating the tragedy. Admiral Kerrins had decided to reconvene the inquiry into the *Bradley's* sinking in the *Sundew's* tiny wardroom.

Coast Guard Board of Inquiry convenes aboard the *Sundew*
Photo Credit--Detroit Times

One of the first to give testimony was Captain Muth, who described how the search had been conducted and answered questions put to him by the board. The captain described the events of the long night in his usual understated way, treating the extraordinary conditions the *Sundew* had faced as if it was just a normal day's work.

Later, Warren Toussaint was called in. He was asked about the condition of the bodies that were recovered and how they were dressed. Asked if he had any recommendations as to what they might have been done to prevent hypothermia, he had replied, " No." When asked if he had anything he wanted to add, he looked directly at the assembled officers and said, "Yes I do. We would of never made it back if it wasn't for the professionalism of the captain, and the whole crew feels this way." With that, Toussaint left the room. When the Board of Inquiry finished taking statements at the docks, Admiral Kerrins declared they would reconvene at the Charlevoix hospital, later that day.

Back in Rogers City, the Bradley Transportation Company was quietly making arrangements to help families with the expense of the many funerals. Four ships of the company's fleet had docked at Calcite so that their crews could attend the funeral services in town. Relatives of the deceased who were sailors on the other four "Bradley Boats" were flown home by the company to be with their families for the funeral services.

One of the Bradley Company's boats would not be carrying cargo any time soon. The crew of the *Irvin L. Clymer* protested the condition of their ship in a petition to the company, with the result that its departure was postponed, while the U.S. Coast Guard was called in to make an inspection. The *Clymer* had crossed Lake Erie in gale conditions the same night the *Bradley* sank. The petition claimed that the storm aggravated existing cracks in the *Clymer's* hull, and it was taking on so much water that it was necessary to pump two hours out of every four. Christian F. Beukema, president of Michigan Limestone, refused to confirm or deny the petition, but said: "There has been a Coast Guard inspection of the *Clymer,* and the ship will leave port without cargo and go to a shipyard."

In an interesting footnote to the story, the *Irvin L. Clymer* originally carried the name *Carl D. Bradley*. It was renamed the *John G. Munson* when the second *Carl D. Bradley* was built in 1927 and renamed the *Clymer* in 1952.

* * *

The bright sun did little to dispel the gloom that permeated Rogers City on this day. Throughout the town, people prepared themselves to bury 12 of their own, while in nearby Onaway, preparations were being made to lay two more to rest. A day of mourning had been declared by Mayor Vogelheim, and all places of business were closed at the request of the Chamber of Commerce's president, John Minelli. The following proclamation appeared in the <u>Presque Isle County Advance</u>:

> It is with deep sorrow and sympathy that I, Kenneth P. Vogelheim, Mayor, proclaim Saturday, November 22, 1958 the official day of mourning in Rogers City.
>
> May God, in his goodness, give us the grace to bear this sorrow. In faith, family and friends, may the widows and children forever find comfort.
>
> Through the years, our blessings have been many. Ours is truly a community of men who have gone down to the sea in ships. Third generation "sailors" are a part of everyday living. Economically and romantically, we are proud of our marine history, a story unparalled anywhere on the Great Lakes. The *Carl D. Bradley* disaster will forever be a terrible, heartbreaking part of our record.
>
> For 30 days, flags in this community will be flown at half mast. Following this day of mourning, each year, hereafter, the date of November 18th shall be

121

dedicated, in Rogers City, to our loved ones who, on that date, lost their lives.

As over 30 fatherless children rose that morning, few could totally comprehend the tragedy of their situation. Today, they would be saying a final farewell to their fathers, who had so abruptly been taken from them. For many, the reality of the death of their father would not sink in for weeks or even months. That morning, teary-eyed relatives fussed with the children's hair and clothing, while many of their mothers seemed in a daze, unable to focus on all the activity going on around them. Many of the wives seemed lost in a world of disbelief, continually questioning, "How could God have let this happen?"

A number of the families of crewman whose bodies had not been recovered avoided the services that day. They did not want to accept the reality that their loved one was also lost. Several stayed by the phone, still hoping to get a call from the company with word that their man had also survived. It was a slim hope, but it was all they had.

The Knights of Columbus salute the "Lost Sailors"
Photo Credit--The Alpena News

122

The day of mourning began with preparations for the 10:00 AM mass funeral service at St. Ignatius Catholic Church. The Requiem High Mass would honor nine of the faithful: Joseph Krawczak, Raymond Kowalski, Alva Budnick, Gary

Nine caskets fill the center aisle of St. Ignatius Catholic Church
Photo Credit- Presque Isle County Advance

Strzelecki, Alfred Boehmer, William Elliott, Alfred Pilarski, Bernard Schefke and Leo Promo Jr. In the gymnasium next to the church, the families held a private casket closing service, which was attended by hundreds. Sixty pallbearers would carry the nine caskets into the church, where more relatives and friends waited. Over 2,000 people attended the service. A standing room only crowd of 800 mourners waited in the church itself, with another 400 seated in the gymnasium of the adjacent St. Ignatius High School. The overflow of mourners stood outside on Third Street, Rogers City's main thoroughfare, where the service would be heard over loud speakers.

Rogers City was a sailing town, a fact reflected in the construction of the old St. Ignatius church. The interior was built to resemble a ship, symbolizing the faith of the men who made their livelihoods sailing the lakes. The entrance to the church represented the stern, while the altar was at the bow. Round, stained glass windows along the walls took the place of portholes.

When it was time for the service to begin, 60 pallbearers carried the nine caskets from the gymnasium to the church. At the church's entrance, 24 Knights of Columbus in full dress uniform stood tall, creating an arch with their drawn swords through which the pallbearers carried the flag draped caskets. The church bell tolled as the slow procession of caskets trailed by grieving family members made their way into the church. The caskets were placed in the center aisle of the church, and the family members were helped to their seats.

The sermon was delivered by the Bishop of Saginaw, Rev. Stephen S. Woznicki. Father Narloch, a kindly, gray haired man, beloved by the community, spoke next. His comforting words were carried throughout the church as he spoke of the deceased, many of whom he had watched grow from mischievous school boys to men of the lakes. The service lasted nearly 90 minutes, and at the conclusion, a procession of over 300 cars, almost two miles long, followed the nine hearses to the Mt. Calvary Cemetery, five miles southwest of town, where a grave-side service was held. Such were the demands placed on the funeral homes that day, that some of the hearses had been borrowed from undertakers almost 100 miles away.

At 12:00 noon, all work stopped aboard the "Bradley Boats", and memorial services were held on the four boats not in port that day. On each ship, a minister and priest were brought on board to conduct the services. In Ohio, the steamer *M.C. Taylor* was moored at Conneaut. On her

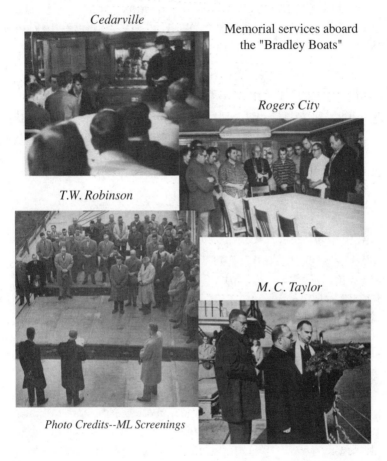

Cedarville

Memorial services aboard the "Bradley Boats"

Rogers City

T.W. Robinson

M. C. Taylor

Photo Credits--ML Screenings

deck, employees from Conneaut joined the *Taylor's* crew in a memorial service. The *T. W. Robinson* was also on Lake Erie at Buffalo, New York. As had happened in Conneaut, the Buffalo Plant employees came on deck and joined the crew of the *Robinson* for the memorial service held there. The crew of the Steamer *Rogers City* held their service on Lake Michigan at South Chicago, while the *Cedarville* held service at Port Huron, at the southern end of Lake Huron.

Saturday afternoon, Father Narloch held another service at the McWilliams Funeral Home, this one for Edward N. Vallee. After family, relatives, and friends had paid their final respects, Edward Vallee was brought to Mt. Calvary Cemetery to join the nine that were buried there earlier that day.

At 1:30 PM, Rev. Robert Weller of St. John's Lutheran Church began the service for Paul Heller. During the service, he quoted one of Heller's favorite passages from the bible, "If God be for us, who can be against us." Rev. Weller praised Paul Heller for the hard work he had put into the church when he was in port and said that he would be truly missed.

A couple of hours later, St. John's was again filled to capacity as Rev. Weller began the services for Paul Horn. As with the earlier service for Paul Heller, the church was filled with the sound of some of the favorite hymns of the deceased, including "Jesus Pilot Me." Both men were buried in the Rogers City Memorial Cemetery.

* * *

While mourners were paying their last respects to the known dead from the *Bradley's* crew, Coast Guard helicopters and search planes continued to hunt for survivors and wreckage. Crewmen of one of the Coast Guard Search planes spotted an oil slick over the surface of Lake Michigan near where the *Bradley* was thought to have sunk, and a surface vessel was dispatched to collect a sample.

As night fell, word came that the hunt for survivors was officially terminated, with the exception of a Coast Guard plane that would make low passes over the islands near the sinking for the next few days.

In order to question the survivors, Admiral Kerrins had reconvened the board of inquiry in the solarium of the

126

Charlevoix Hospital. Elmer Fleming was the first to be brought in, accompanied by Cleveland marine attorney, Roman T. Keenen. Keenan explained that he had been retained in the event that any charges were brought that could cause Mr. Fleming to lose his certificate.

The proceedings began at 7:00 PM and lasted for nearly two hours. Elmer spoke clearly, although his voice was often filled with emotion. As his story unfolded, his delivery quickened, and he spoke at length before taking questions.

Elmer gave a detailed, step-by-step, account of the actions of the captain and crew from the time the *Bradley* left Gary until the rescue. His statements to the board of inquiry were consistent with what he had told Captain Muth the day he was rescued.

Asked to elaborate on the actions of Captain Bryan, Elmer told the board that Captain Bryan had asked the cooks to serve an early dinner the night the *Bradley* sank. He knew the turn from Lake Michigan toward Lake Huron would put the heavy weather broadside of the ship. He wanted to give the mess crew a chance to get everything cleaned up after dinner and be able to secure the galley before the turn. Elmer also added that, in the mess room, the men were joking, as they were eager to get home. They even took down the side rails that had been put up at the tables to prevent the plates from slipping off, saying that these aren't needed.

Elmer told them that at 5:26 PM, he was in radio contact with Rogers City. The company had called to tell him that one of the *Bradley's* crewmembers, who happened to be in Rogers City at that time, would be joining the ship's crew on the next trip. He reported that this conversation took place just minutes before he had heard the loud thud that signaled the start of the *Bradley's* breakup. When asked how the captain had responded to the danger, Elmer told how Captain Bryan had immediately sounded the general alarm and grabbed the chadburn and threw it into the stop position, notifying the engine crew to stop the ship. He then blew the whistle to signal the crew to abandon ship.

At that point, a physician called a halt to the interview, stating that Elmer seemed fatigued and that the board would have to continue its inquiry at another time.

Prior to the board interviews of the survivors, Victor Hanson, an attorney out of Detroit, presented himself to the board as the legal representative of the widows of John Fogelsonger, Raymond Kowalski, Gary Strzelecki, and Earl Tulgetske, Jr. Hanson asked for permission to interview the survivors. The Bradley Transportation Company's lawyers objected on the grounds that the inquiry was not a court trial. Admiral Kerrins, in his role as head of the inquiry, ruled that Mr. Hanson could submit written questions.

Some of the questions that the families sought answers to were about the hull plates that were found cracked during the *Bradley's* last drydock inspection and about their repair. Other questions were about the lifeboat drills and whether they were done as required. During the inquiry, it was stated that the lifeboat drills were done regularly and had been inspected by the U.S. Coast Guard.

17 *Sunday*

Frank remembers his turn before the board of inquiry:

As dawn broke that Sunday morning, I was up eating breakfast and thinking about the testimony I was scheduled to give that day. I wasn't nervous about the meeting, it would be easy. All I had to do is tell them exactly what happened.

It was pretty quiet as I was wheeled into the Solarium that morning. The sunshine filled the room, a scene quite different from the last time I was in there answering questions.

I was duly sworn in by Lieutenant Commander Garth H. Read, the recorder for the board. He said, "State your name and home address."

So I rattled it off. He then asked me about my sailing experience, including what I had done in the Navy. They were simple questions, and I gave simple short answers.

Then he got into questions about the ballast of the ship. Lieutenant Commander Read asked, "Did you know how much water was in on the eighteenth?"

I replied, "I pumped it in."

I knew he was drilling me about the ballast of the ship, because if a ship is too light in heavy seas, then it can break up. I told him the amount I was told to put in.

Lieutenant Commander Read then asked, "Is that the maximum ballast in the vessel you have ever seen?"

I quickly replied, "Yes." I kept my answers short, and I didn't elaborate on the details.

He moved on to questions of the how the ship was riding when I came on duty.

I told them, "I would say normal for what the seas were."

When the questions got to the sinking, I elaborated a little more. I wanted to make sure they knew what happened. I told them about how I was thrown into the water.

Even though Lieutenant Commander Read asked most of the questions, the other members of the board did interrupt with questions now and then.

Lieutenant Commander Read asked, "Would you have liked to have had a flashlight?"

I replied, "Yes."

He continued, "How about a light on the lifejackets."

I responded, "That would help. If you went off the raft someone could see you."

He asked, "You could of picked somebody else up?"

I answered, "Yes, we couldn't get to anybody, though."

At the end of the inquiry, the Chairman, Admiral Kerrins asked, "What enabled you to endure the 14-plus hours on the life raft and come through alive?"

I thought for a second, and I replied, "At no time was I ever scared. I prayed, and I had faith in being rescued. I knew we would get picked up when it got daylight. I never gave up hope."

He asked, "Did you do anything to keep yourself going?"

I quickly answered, "We talked until we just didn't feel like talking anymore—we banged until we couldn't bang any more, then just held on."

Shortly after that question, I was happy to hear the words, "You are excused."

Before I went back to my room, we all shook hands, and Elmer and I posed for some pictures with the members of the board.

Elmer and Frank pose with the members of the USCG Board of Inquiry
Photo Credit--Detroit Times

Later that day, Elmer granted an interview with the marine author, William Ratigan, who was later to write the book, Shipwrecks and Survivals. In his interview, Elmer described the seas the night the *Bradley* broke up. "It was as if there were no waves in the middle, but a big one at each end with nothing in between. She just seemed to drop out in the middle."

Another highlight of that interview was Elmer's disclosure that other members of the crew tried to launch the *Bradley's* starboard lifeboat just before she went down. "But the tilt of the ship was so bad by then that they didn't have a chance."

* * *

Sunday had also seen a continuation of services for the lost sailors. The day began with an 11:00 AM memorial service led by Rev. F. T. Steen at the Westminster Presbyterian Church, where Elmer Fleming was a member. At 2:00 PM, Pastor Herbert J. Meyer conducted funeral services for Erhardt Felax at the Gatzke Funeral Home. Simultaneously in the nearby town of Onaway, a funeral service was being held for Cleland Gager. His family and friends paid their last respects in the Holy Cross Lutheran Church, with the Rev. C.F. Bourger officiating. As that service finished, another began at the nearby Karr Funeral Chapel, where services were held for Gary Price. Elder Ernest N. Burt officiated, as relatives and friends filled the Chapel. Cleland Gager and Gary Price were both buried in South Allis Cemetery.

18 *Monday*

Another day, another funeral. St. Mary's Church in Cheboygan was the scene Monday morning of a funeral mass for John Bauers, one of the *Bradley's* engineers. Even though his body had not yet been found, his family wished to have a service for him. Bauers and his wife Aileen, along with their two young sons, Mark and Jerry, were living in Rogers City at the time of his death. However, his funeral service was held in Cheboygan, where he had spent his childhood.

At about the same time in Traverse City, the board of inquiry convened and took testimony in regards to the search operations conducted by the Coast Guard aircraft from Traverse City and elsewhere. Nothing new was learned and Admiral Kerrins stated, "It is difficult to get anything factual on the cause of the sinking of the lake freighter, since there are only two survivors, and the boat is under some 300 feet of water."

Their initial inquiries completed, the officers of the board of investigation flew back to Cleveland, where they would begin the job of sorting through the information they had collected. It would be some months before they released their findings.

* * *

Frank has a special reason to celebrate:

Monday, November 24 was a special day for me for a number of reasons. Not only was I alive and feeling much better, but today was my 27th birthday. My parents, Frank and Mary, came to the hospital, along with my wife and our good friends, Enos and Janette Brege. They brought me a cake, and it was a real treat, especially having my friends and family near. After they had gone, I just lay in bed and thought how really lucky I was to be alive.

Life in the hospital wasn't bad at all. They treated us great. If I were to rate our time there on a scale from one to ten, it would have been a thousand and ten. We could have anything we wanted within reason. There was even a guy who owned a store that sold televisions that came and put a TV in our room and an antenna up outside our window so we could get better reception. Yeah, we were treated like kings, but I was still glad I was leaving on Wednesday, so I could get back home to see my boys.

I had a lot of time to myself to think while I was in the hospital. I was going home Wednesday, and Thursday was Thanksgiving. Then, it all came back to me. Just last week, Elmer and I were talking in the *Bradley's* pilothouse about being home for Thanksgiving and whether we would make it in time. The memory dampened my spirits. Elmer and I were coming home for Thanksgiving, but just Elmer and me.

19 *Thanksgiving*

Thanksgiving was a very difficult time for the families of the *Bradley's* lost crew. The empty places at the dinner table were a stark reminder of their missing men, and many wondered just what they had to give thanks for. As more fortunate families sat down to the traditional feast, many were asking themselves what they could do to help the grieving families. From across the state and nation, letters poured in,

Captains of the Bradley Fleet hold several of the children made fatherless by the sinking
Photo Credit--ML Screenings

many with donations to the *Carl D. Bradley* Disaster Fund. As of that Thanksgiving, the fund had swelled to $25,000, a respectable sum in 1958. The Bradley Transportation Company itself had recently given a $10,000 donation. Newspapers still encouraged readers to give donation and printed the names of contributors. There were also other modest funds started throughout the state. One example was

Vernon Scott of Alpena, who collected over $300 at his ice cream parlor.

By the end of 1958, the *Carl D*. *Bradley* Disaster Fund totaled over $154,000. Michigan Limestone Division had donated $10,000 early in the campaign. The Michigan Limestone Division employees, themselves, contributed nearly $23,000. Included in that total was $9,140, donated by the crews of the other ships in the Bradley fleet. Crews from other lake vessels also helped out, collecting over $18,000. Customers and associates of U.S. Steel and the Bradley Transportation Company donated another $15,543. Pleased with the success of the collection effort, the fund's trustees reported:

> "Fifty-two eligible children will receive equal shares in the fund, with the wife of one *Bradley* victim expecting another child.
>
> Trustees have enrolled the children in a group health insurance plan, the cost to be paid by the fund's earnings. The Trustees, who serve without pay, have invested $100,000 of the money in U.S. Government bonds and the rest in three per cent savings certificates. Cash will be available to help children as needed. Money remaining in each child's share of the fund will be paid as they reach 21 years of age."

> *ML Screenings, Winter Issue 1958-59*

20 *Many Questions, Few Answers*

The Coast Guard reconvened the *Bradley* inquiry on Tuesday, December 2, 1958, at the Courthouse in Rogers City. The courtroom was filled with townspeople and family members of those lost on the *Carl D. Bradley*. Michael Idalski, third assistant engineer, testified to repair work done on the *Bradley*, which had been ordered and completed satisfactorily. Sylvester Sobeck, first assistant engineer of the *Carl D. Bradley*, also testified as to repair work that had been ordered and had been carried out (Sylvester was the fortunate sailor who missed the *Bradley's* last trip because of his brother's funeral). When questioned in regard to the grounding of the *Bradley* at Cedarville earlier that fall, Robert Leow and Norman Hoeft testified briefly about the damage done to the hull plates and the repairs that were made.

At the close of the hearing, Rear Admiral Kerrins spoke up and said that, if there were any witnesses in the room that could offer any more facts regarding the sinking, they would be heard. Mrs. Earl Tulgetske spoke up, declaring that the *Bradley* did not conduct regular lifeboat drills. The gist of her comments to the Board of Inquiry and the Admiral's reply were recorded in the Presque Isle County Advance on Thursday, December 4, 1958.

Mrs. Earl Tulgetske protested that the *Bradley* did not have regular lifeboat drills, that her husband had told her the men did not know which way to turn when drills were called,

137

and that they were not orderly, and made other statements contradicting the testimony that had been offered.

Rear Admiral Kerrins expressed concern for her feelings and for the feelings of others who have suffered in the disaster. He was very patient and very understanding, but was firm in his decision that the Board of Inquiry could not accept, for the record, anything but factual evidence. It was on this note that the inquiry was closed.

* * *

One of the issues hampering the inquiry into the loss of the Bradley *was the fact that her final resting place had not been determined, and the ship itself had not been examined. Because of his close association with the* Bradley *sinking and rescue, Captain Harold Muth recalls how he decided to do a little investigating on his own:*

Later in December, we were out pulling in our buoys for the winter from the vicinity of Boulder Reef. Since we were out there anyway, we made a few runs to see whether or not we could pick up the wreck of the *Bradley*. After making a few passes, we discovered something on the bottom about five miles northwest of the Boulder Reef that looked like it might be the silhouette of a large vessel.

We had a recording Fathometer, which used a stylus to record a drawing of the outline of the bottom on a roll of graph paper. We had the Fathometer in operation as we crossed over the site, and we recorded the silhouette of something that looked like a large ship. We took note of the position and saved the recording, which I then sent to Cleveland. I never heard anything about it afterwards.

In the month of February, 1959, the Cleveland headquarters asked us to join with the Cutter *Mackinaw* and to search for

138

the *Bradley*. However, the ice conditions were so heavy that search efforts were futile.

* * *

In the early spring, the ice had cleared enough to allow the hunt for the *Bradley* to continue. Donald T. Nauts, a senior captain of the Bradley Line, began his search in the area near Boulder Reef. He was using a sonar device, called a *Sea Scanar* which sent high frequency sound waves toward the lake bottom and then recorded their echoes as the sound waves bounced back. The *Sea Scanar* produced tracings on a chart that showed the contour of the bottom. After several

The *Submarex* expedition examined the *Bradley* in 1959

Photo Credit--ML Screenings

passes over the area, Captain Nauts and his crew located what he thought was the *Bradley*, lying on the lake bottom in 360 feet of water.

Based upon the tracings collected by Captain Nauts, U.S. Steel announced that the *Bradley* was in one piece lying on the

139

bottom. According to a statement in the company's magazine, ML Screenings (Fall 1959), "While it was generally believed that the *Bradley* sank in two pieces, the sonar tracing showed that she appeared in one piece."

The admiralty law firms representing the Bradley Transportation Company then hired Global Marine Exploration Company of Los Angeles to make a study of the wreck site. To do this, the 175-foot motor vessel, *Submarex*, was brought from the west coast thru the Panama Canal, up the east coast, and through the St. Lawrence Seaway to the Great Lakes. Aboard the *Submarex* was underwater television equipment ordinarily used for working on offshore oil wells. According to an article in the company's magazine, the *Submarex* made "an extensive ten-day examination of the *Bradley*. Positive identification was made by reading the name, *Carl D. Bradley*, on a television monitor screen." The article continued to say, "The ship was reported to have continuity of the lower hull section, confirming the earlier sonar findings that the object was in one piece. While breaks in the deck area were found, the rest of the hull appeared to be sound and in excellent condition." *ML Screenings, Fall Issue, 1959.*

The Bradley Transportation Company also claimed they had photographs from that expedition that proved their assertion that the *Bradley* was in one piece. These pictures were never made public, even when lawyers requested them in a lawsuit.

* * *

Author's note: We have reliable evidence that the pictures did indeed exist from the family of the man who developed them. This man never revealed their contents, carrying their secrets to his grave.

Captain Muth's Final Thoughts:

There was a board of investigation, where it was determined that the *Bradley* broke up in heavy seas due to what they called a hogging condition. This is where extra tall waves roll underneath a ship and because of the heavy weight on each end, the ship breaks in half.

I think there has always been some concern over whether the *Bradley* broke in heavy seas or whether something else contributed to its sinking. The board's official finding was that she broke up in heavy seas.

After an incident like this, one always has second thoughts about whether or not the measures you took, the search efforts and so forth were the best that could have been done. When you look at the wind conditions, the sea conditions, the cold temperatures, and the almost complete absence of any wreckage, you cannot come up with a good answer. I think the sinking of the *Carl D. Bradley*, the sinking of the *Daniel J. Morrell*, and the sinking of the *Edmond Fitzgerald*, all of which broke in half in heavy storms, in Lake Michigan, Lake Huron, and Lake Superior, leave us with many, many questions and not too many answers.

Note: See the full text of the Coast Guard's "Commandant's Action" and "Finding of Fact" in the Appendix section of this book.

21 *A New Life on Shore*

Frank describes life after the Bradley:

When I first got home from the hospital, my neighbors from across the street, Enos and Janette Brege, came over to visit all the time. They were good friends. Another time, I was shoveling snow, and a neighbor from down the street stopped by to talk. Other than those few, only Dick Newhouse, a man I sailed with on the *Clymer*, ever came over to talk to me. I appreciated Dick's visits. He lived in the neighborhood where I grew up. Even though he and his brothers and sisters were much older than I was, I knew them well, because they were always walking by. I don't know why the others avoided me. Had I done something wrong by surviving?

The only U.S. Steel representative to come to the house was Harry McHarg. He brought me a check for $300 to cover loss of personal property. Otherwise, U.S. Steel never bothered with me. Today, you'd have counselors to help you get through things, but they did nothing. Well, that's not entirely true. They did visit us at the hospital, and they picked us up from Charlevoix and gave us a ride to Rogers City. All things considered, I don't think U.S. Steel treated us very well, especially me.

After the sinking, I had no desire to go back sailing. The company said that I didn't have to, and they gave me a job shuffling papers at the storehouse. Rogers City was a company town of U.S. Steel, and it was obvious that they wanted to hush the sinking up as much as they possibly could. Around town, you wouldn't hear much said about it, but you can bet it was on the minds of the wives, mothers, fathers, and relatives of men who were lost. This led to an uncomfortable situation when I ran into them in stores or on the street. What could I say? Seeing me was a painful reminder that their loved one had not returned. With that in mind, I thought it might be a good idea for Marlys and I to go stay with her parents in Waterloo, Iowa for awhile, and the company agreed.

When I came home from Iowa, I began work at the company storehouse in Rogers City. I worked there for almost a year until, on New Years Eve, 1959, they told me I had to go back sailing. They said there was no more work for me in a shore job. I think it was their way of firing me, without actually giving me the boot, because they knew I wouldn't go back on the boats.

It is my personal opinion that the reason for the company's action was related to events that took place after I was called to Cleveland to testify about the sinking. The company's attorney, Roman Keenen, took me aside and told me he would represent me at no charge. He told me not to put a claim in, saying, "You're not going to get anything, because you are a survivor, and there is nothing in the pot for you. We will represent you and take care of all of your problems."

Something told me that the company might not have my best interests at heart, so I decided to speak to one of the other attorneys I saw at the hearing. Ken Davies was his name, and when I saw him later in the day, I told him, "I want to talk to you." He asked me where I was staying, so I gave him the name of the hotel. He told me to go back to my room, and he would send a cab for me. So Marlys and I went back to our room. Sure enough, when I got back there, I got a phone call from the front desk telling me a taxi was waiting for me.

I wasted no time going down to the cab, which drove me to a restaurant where I met the attorney. We discussed the *Bradley* and what the company lawyer had advised me, and I soon realized I would be better off with my own representation. I said, "Ken you're my attorney."

To which he replied, "Good."

He announced to U.S. Steel that he was representing me, and after that is when they came around and told me I had no more work. They didn't say I was fired, they just said you have no more work. I guess I would term the experience as being "politely" fired.

My older brother, Harry, had an airplane. He worked in Detroit, and he would fly between Detroit and Rogers City. He was going back to Detroit on the Sunday night after I got fired, so I asked him, "Will you give me a ride to Detroit? I'm going down to see Christian Beukema, the headman of U.S. Steel in the Detroit office. I'm going to find out why they fired me!"

So, he flew me down to Detroit, and I stayed in his apartment for a couple of days. On Monday, I went to the offices of U.S. Steel and told the girls who I was and why I was there. Mr. Beukema would not see me. I stayed in that office all day long. At the end of the day, he wouldn't come out, or anything. I just wanted to know why they fired me, but Christian Beukema did not have the integrity to tell me to my face. Somehow, he had found the gumption to say, on tape, that the *Bradley* never broke in two. His claim that it was in one piece on the bottom of the lake was something that I knew was absolutely untrue. I was there, he wasn't. Even so, he had the nerve to comment that I was too young and didn't understand what actually happened. That angered me, because I know what happened that night. It will forever be burned in my mind.

144

Back in Rogers City, I worked doing winter lay-up work on the boats for about two weeks while I looked for a new job. Leo Bruski, who owned a lumber company in Posen, Michigan, offered me a job, which I started in February of 1960.

Not only did the sinking have an effect on my job, it had an effect on my first marriage. Shortly after the birth of Kimberly on July 10, 1961, Marlys and I divorced.

* * *

While I was working for the lumber company, I met Veronica Derry. Called Toodie by her family, I met her while visiting my brother at Grand Lake. We dated for a while and then got married in Centerline, Michigan. On March 30, 1963, we were blessed with the birth of our son, Eric Matthew. Then on September 22, 1964, our daughter, Laine Marie, was born.

In May of 1967, I left the Bruski Lumber Company and went to work for the Medusa Cement Company in Charlevoix, Michigan. We moved to Charlevoix, where I bought a farm. I had always wanted to be a farmer, and it was a happy time in my life. I had a wonderful job and a great home life. I remember a family trip where we traveled out west, pulling a pop-up camper. We went up to the Soo Locks and then through Canada to the west.

In 1975, Medusa Cement transferred me to York, Pennsylvania. I became the office manager, and I enjoyed that position too. While we were there, I would take the family on vacations to the east coast. As a family, we did enjoy traveling.

Medusa transferred me again in 1982, to Brooksville, Florida. There, I worked as a purchasing agent. I enjoyed Florida and decided to make it my home. Toodie and I built a beautiful house in Spring Hill and had our own orange, tangerine, banana, and grapefruit trees.

I retired from Medusa Cement in 1990 at the age of 58. I soon got bored and went to work at a nursing home, where Toodie worked as a nurse's aid, and I worked as a maintenance man. I was only going to work for a couple of years, but I liked it so well, I stayed there.

During 1993, Toodie and I traveled all over Europe. We were in Holland, Germany, Austria, Switzerland, Italy, France, and Belgium. We had a great trip.

* * *

I'd never really forgotten the *Bradley,* but years had passed, and I had made a new life for myself. Then, out of nowhere, Port Huron artist Jim Clary called me and he said that there was a chance I could go and make a dive to the *Bradley* in a submarine. I was excited at the prospect and said, "Absolutely, I'll do it!" As the day of the dive approached, I made my way up to Rogers City, where I visited for a while before leaving to meet the sub crew in Cheboygan. It was August 10, 1995 when I saw the sub for the first time and met the rest of the crew. In addition to Clary and his partner Fred Shannon, I met Bernie Hellstrom, who had relocated the *Bradley* and Rick Mixter, a television producer.

Clary and Shannon decided that I would do a practice dive on the wreck of the *Cedarville* (in the Straits of Mackinac) to see how I was going to do in the sub. I guess they were concerned that I might panic or something. They needn't have worried. I enjoyed the dive and appreciated the chance to see the *Cedarville*, which I had briefly sailed on.

Leaving the straits, we proceeded on to Lake Michigan and Charlevoix. The weather was bad, and it took a long time to get the boat to Charlevoix, but we got in there for the night. The next morning, we went out to the *Bradley* site and got situated. Bernie Hellstrom had been the first to relocate the *Bradley* since the *Submarex* expedition in 1959. For 36 years, the *Bradley* had lain, forgotten, on the bottom of Lake Michigan. Bernie managed to drop a weighted line on the *Bradley,* which would guide the sub in the limited visibility.

Fred Shannon made the first trip, but all he saw was some debris. When it was my turn, the sub was able to follow the guideline all the way to the *Bradley's* starboard side, where we landed right on the deck near the after end. The pilot raised the sub up over the railing and dropped down until we sat right on the bottom of Lake Michigan. We were right alongside of the *Bradley*, but where? As we started to come up, we spotted the name, *CARL D. BRADLEY*, which was on the stern section on the starboard side. Drifting back over on the deck, we dropped a plaque bearing the names of the crewmembers and some information. Then, we tried to follow the side of the ship, but the visibility was not very good. We could see only two or three feet at the most, so we had to stay so close that we were literally scraping the side of the ship. At one point, we got too far away and fearing that we might blunder into some cables and get caught, the pilot decided it was time to return to the surface. We were down there about 25 minutes, and we had the video cameras on the whole time. There was no doubt that this was the *Carl D. Bradley.*

In 1997, I went out again with Jim Clary and Fred Shannon to explore the *Bradley.* This time, we had a remotely operated vehicle (ROV) that was sent down while we stayed up on the mother ship. We had monitors that showed us everything the ROV saw. We examined both the stern and the bow section. One of the men that operated this ROV determined that the two pieces were approximately 120 feet apart. You could actually see the space between the two sections. So, it was definitely two pieces on the bottom. It is lying upright. Not perfectly upright, the sections have a list to port. The forward

147

section is deep into the mud up to the boom, but the bow is at such an angle that it is clear underneath. In fact, you could probably walk under it if you had to.

The stern section is stuck in the mud at such an angle that the propeller and rudder are also very visible.

Seeing the *Bradley* in such detail made me feel good, real good. U.S. Steel wanted the world to believe that the *Bradley* never broke into two pieces, and ridiculed my claim to the contrary. It was with great satisfaction that I was able to say, "I saw it in two pieces on the surface, and now I've seen it in two pieces on the bottom of Lake Michigan." You can't argue with the facts.

* * *

November 1998 marked the 40th anniversary of the *Bradley's* sinking. I was contacted by Jim Stayer of <u>Out of the Blue Productions</u> and asked if I was willing to participate in a special remembrance of the *Bradley* to be held in Port Huron. I was a little suspicious of their motives, but in checking around, I learned they were well regarded as shipwreck documentary producers and authors. Their first *Shipwrecks Remembered* program had been staged in 1996, where the story of the *Daniel J. Morrell*, which sank in Lake Huron in 1966, was featured. Sole survivor, Dennis Hale, had been the main speaker, and the event had concluded with a solemn bell ceremony where a ship's bell was rung as the names of the crew were called out. The event had brought closure to many of the families of the *Morrell's* crew, who had felt that their loved ones were forgotten. I hoped they would be able to do the same for the *Bradley*.

Inasmuch as it was 40 years later, I was happy that someone wanted to honor the *Bradley*. One television station had described her as, "The *Carl D. Bradley*, the ship that time forgot." Every November, you heard about the loss of the *Fitzgerald*, but nothing about the *Bradley*. As it turned out, the program was very well presented, and I was grateful to have the chance to tell my story. It was also wonderful to see Captain Muth of the *Sundew* again, and thank him once more for rescuing me. I'd never really had a chance to hear him tell his side of the story, which he delivered that night in that modest way of his. Dennis Hale was there, and I

Dennis Hale, Captain Harold Muth, Jim Stayer, Tim Juhl,
Pat Stayer, and Frank Mays at Shipwrecks Remembered 1998
Photo Credit--Cris Kohl

appreciated the chance to talk to someone who could relate to my experiences when the *Bradley* sank. We also had a bell ceremony for the *Bradley's* crew that night, which I was honored to be a part of. Since that time, I have enjoyed a close relationship with Jim and Pat Stayer and their partner, Tim Juhl. I greatly appreciate their assistance in making this book a reality.

Unfortunately, a short time after the show in Port Huron, my wife, Toodie, passed away. I felt all alone, so I thought it was best for me to stay at my nursing home job for awhile, even though I had originally planned to retire at the end of 1998.

In April of 1999, I retired from the nursing home after being there for nine years. It wasn't long before I was bored again, so I decided to join the Peace Corps.

While I was waiting for my Peace Corps paperwork to be processed, I had the opportunity to return to the Great Lakes and sail aboard a Great Lakes freighter. It would be the first time I sailed on the Great Lakes in 42 years. Dennis Hale, the sole survivor from the *Daniel J. Morrell*, had been offered the chance to take a trip on the *MV Roger Blough* with seven of his friends. He invited Jim & Pat Stayer and Tim & Joan Juhl from Out of the Blue Productions, folksinger Dan Hall, and Harvey "Batman" Hays. Dennis and Harvey had roomed together on the *Daniel J. Morrell* the year before it sank. For the remaining guest, Jim suggested that Dennis invite me. That way, we could have a survivor reunion.

In late July, we joined the *Blough* at the Soo and sailed across lake Superior to Two Harbors, Minnesota, to pick up a load of taconite for Gary, Indiana. Crossing Lake Superior again, we went back through the locks into Lake Huron and under the Mackinaw Bridge into Lake Michigan. That is when I had a chance to fulfill one of my life-long dreams. I had always wanted to wheel a freighter under the Mackinac Bridge, and Captain Larry "Duke" Dahlgren gave me my chance. Later, when we departed Gary on our return to the Soo, I couldn't help but remember the last time I had done so on what was to be the *Bradley's* final, fatal, voyage. It was a somber moment. The ironic part of sailing aboard the *Blough*

Dennis Hale and Frank Mays aboard the *MV Roger Blough* at the Soo
Photo Credit- Pat Stayer

was that the ship was part of the U.S. Steel fleet, and here I was getting the royal treatment after being fired many years earlier. I went with a wonderful group and had a tremendous time. We even wrote a song together.

* * *

In the fall of 1999, I received my training for the Peace Corps and was sent to serve in the small country of Moldova, which used to be part of the Soviet Union. I spent six months there, during which I did a lot of traveling. I went to Belarus, Romania, Ukraine, Georgia, and throughout Moldova. I really enjoyed the people, but I was glad to return to the United States.

I had such a good experience overseas that I decided to stay in retirement and travel around the world. My first trip was to China and Indonesia. I was gone for four weeks.

In the next two years, I traveled extensively, visiting Turkey, Thailand, Laos, Egypt, Sri Lanka, Taiwan, Japan, and Burma (Myanmar).

151

In the summer of 2001, I returned to the Great Lakes again. Captain J.R. Parsons of the *MV St. Clair*, a personal friend of mine, invited me on a six-day trip. We went from Lake Erie to Lake Superior and back. I had a great time.

Later that year, I went to South America and visited Peru and later, the Central American country of Costa Rica. In July of 2002, I decided to return to Moldova. I flew into Budapest, Hungry, rented a car and drove across Hungry, Romania, and into Moldova. I spent the month of July driving across Moldova, visiting all the families I lived with and some of the friends I'd made when I was there with the Peace Corps.

In the March of 2003, I went to Israel in the company of a close friend. It was a cool day when we visited the Dead Sea, so only three of the five in our group went swimming. It is true that you can't sink in it! We tried to sit in the water, but you couldn't. You just kept rolling over. We ate lunch on the shores of Galilee, and we actually ate fish called Peter fish, named after Saint Peter. In Jerusalem, we walked through the *Stations of the Cross*. We visited a lot of cathedrals and went in the tomb where Jesus was laid after he was taken down from the cross. We spent eight days in Israel and from there, we flew to Cairo, Egypt, where we spent three days. We left Cairo and flew south to Luxor.

When I knew we would be going to Luxor, I wrote a letter to a young fellow I had met when I was in Egypt with the Peace Corps in 2000. I had met this young fellow, Jam Uri Aqmhed Omar Kaliff, who had a felucca (small boat), which he used to take people on the Nile. He is Nubian, a tribe out of southern Egypt, and he lives on the west bank of Luxor. I had dinner in his home and told him that, if I ever came back to Egypt, I would look him up, so he gave me his address. We met up again, and he took my traveling companion and

I on his felucca, which he called *Humpty Dumpty*. We went quite a ways up the Nile before turning back. Along the way, he called his mother on his cell phone, and she had a nice dinner waiting for us when we returned. We sat on the dirt floor in their home and our dinner was put on a tray. We ate with our fingers and enjoyed a wonderful meal. It was quite an experience for my companion. We spent the day with our Egyptian friend and later that evening, went back aboard our cruise ship, which took us up the Nile to the Aswan Dam. The cruise took about ten days and then we returned home.

What can I tell you? Life is good. In my lifetime I've had more experiences than most people, and I'm far from finished. As of this writing I've visited 62 countries and will be going to Italy, Sicily, and Cuba in the not distant future. Take my advice, life is a precious gift and should be enjoyed to the fullest.

—Frank Mays, April 2018—

CAPT. ROLAND BRYAN

THE 33 MEN THAT WENT DOWN WITH THE
CARL D. BRADLEY

EARL TULGETSKE

PAUL GREENGTSKI

PAUL HELLER

MARTIN ENOS

ERHARDT FELAX

JOHN FOGELSONGER

RAY BUEHLER

BERNARD SCHEFKE

FLOYD MacDOUGALL

ALVA BUDNICK

ALFRED BOEHMER

MIKE JOPPICH

KEITH SCHULER

EDWARD VALLEE

JOSEPH KRAWCZAK

RAYMOND KOWALSKI

154

DOUGLAS BELLMORE   JOHN BAUERS   CARL BARTELL   ALFRED PILARSKI

MELVIN ORR   GARY STRZELECKI   LEO PROMO   WILLIAM ELLIOTT

RICHARD BOOK   JAMES SELKE   DUANE BERG   JOHN ZOHO

DENNIS MEREDITH   CLELAND GAGER   GARY PRICE   PAUL HORN

Appendix A.

The *Bradley* Relocated

Bernie Hellstrom, an electrical contractor and commercial diver, was the first person to relocate the *Carl D. Bradley* since the *Submarex* expedition of 1959. Bernie's help was invaluable to both the Deep Quest expeditions in 1995 & 1997 and the subsequent operations conducted by <u>Out of the Blue Productions</u>.

Bernie tells it this way:

My long fascination with the *Bradley* began with the stories told by my dad, Len Hellstrom. When I was a kid he told me about listening to the *Bradley* rescue on a Hallicrafter's shortwave radio while at hunting camp. We lived in Grosse Pointe, Michigan, at the time and he and my uncles had a camp on Black Lake in Onaway. One stormy night while keeping warm in their 20 x 20 foot cabin, they turned on the short wave radio to check on the weather. They wanted to know whether they would get out hunting the next day. Although they missed the "Mayday" call itself, the radio chatter from the rescue efforts captivated them. All through the night they listened.

I became enthralled with shipwrecks and began diving in 1969. Someone gave me a copy of a book by William Ratigan for my birthday. It was called <u>Great Lakes Shipwrecks and Survivals</u>, and it really sparked my interest.

I guess I was always interested in the *Carl D. Bradley*. It was the one shipwreck that nobody looked for or cared about. It was too far out and too deep to dive. After I moved to

Charlevoix, I spent some time researching where the *Bradley* was supposed to be and then went searching for it with a depth sounder. When we had the chance, we would go out and make a dive or two and then if the weather was good, we would go out searching. Otherwise we would work on the lighthouse at Squaw Island. Restoring lighthouses is another love I have.

In 1992, we did a lot of searching to the west of Beaver Island, off Gull Island and Boulder Reef. We were looking for three different wrecks, but the *Bradley* in particular. We had a lot of sonar hits, some of which were in deep water. Some of the hits matched the *Bradley's* depth and her expected height off the bottom, but we had no way of checking these targets out. We just kept the numbers and the paper graph thinking one day they might come in handy.

Curiosity eventually got the better of me so I bought a closed circuit TV surveillance camera system and put it into a homemade underwater housing. It had to be inexpensive, because there was a good chance it would get snagged on the wreck and I would lose it. The system worked well and was even written up in Popular Science Magazine.

In 1995, my son Andy and I went out to the coordinates of the target we'd found and sent the camera down. We got video of a ship's stern rail and a debris field with a lot of parts laying in it. We could see it was a large steel ship, but there was nothing we could use to identify it as the *Bradley*. Another time I took Josh Barnes out with me and again we were only able to find some debris.

Andy and I had better luck when went back to the site on August 4, 1995. It was foggy and visibility that day was really poor, but the lake was calm so we had a better chance of finding the target. After a few passes we found the wreck right where it should have been.

When we lowered the camera down this time we got a view of the side of a ship complete with a porthole. As we came up across the rear deck and to the stern house we were able to

Bernie Hellstrom and his drop camera
Photo Credit--Popular Science

confirm that we had a large freighter. Although we only had a few feet of visibility, we were able to verify that we were looking at the *Bradley* because of the color scheme. When my camera came up on a companionway, I was sure we had finally found the resting place of the *Carl D. Bradley*.

Andy and I went out several more times and got more video of the wreck. We found the best time for us to go to the site was at midnight because the lake was calmer and we could see the television screen better. We used lighted buoys to help position our boat. The wreck of the *Bradley* is a 52-mile run from Charlevoix, so we had to pick the right weather. Each time we headed out, we had to be real careful about our fuel supply because the *Bradley* was at my boat's maximum range. For safety I carried two extra tanks of gas strapped to my swim platform.

Later in 1995, I helped the Deep Quest Expedition locate the site, so they could take a submersible vehicle down to the *Carl D. Bradley*. My daughter, Dianna, came with me. We used my drop camera to make sure we were on the site.

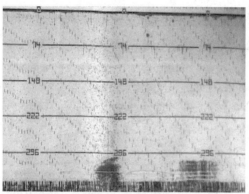

Graph paper showing the *Carl D. Bradley*
Photo Credit--Bernie Hellstrom

Then we dropped my anchor line down to use as a guideline. Because the visibility was so poor, the plan was to have the sub follow this line down to the wreck. Using my camera system a second time, we verified that the down line was indeed on the wreck. My guideline is the reason that when Frank went down in the sub; he was able to land on the deck of the *Bradley*. In fact, my boat line and my anchor are still down there, hooked into the starboard rail of the stern house. I saw it on camera when I went with the expedition in 1997. Deep Quest was using a ROV to video the *Bradley* and on one of the passes we came across it. I asked them to grab it but of course they couldn't. That expedition was able to capture about 26 hours of video footage.

I was pleased that I was able to relocate the *Carl D. Bradley*, and glad that Frank Mays was able to return to her decks once again.

Appendix B.

First SCUBA Dives on the *Bradley*

On August 7, 2001 at 11:04 AM, Mirek Standowicz descended 320 feet beneath the surface of Lake Michigan to become the first person to touch the pilothouse of the freighter *Carl D. Bradley* since its tragic sinking.

Mirek, a certified scuba diver since 1982, had completed over 1,000 dives. Including a number using trimix, a mixture of helium, oxygen and nitrogen. Trimix allows divers to dive deeper with a greater degree of safety.

Mirek's preparation for diving the *Bradley* began in July of 1999. He made over 90 training dives, the deepest to 349 feet. In December of 2000, Mirek recruited two safety divers, Terry Crawford and Natalie Rabidue. Together they made 43 dives, including: ice diving, high current diving, wreck diving, dives exceeding 100 feet and dives that required technical skills. In addition, for eight months, the trio went to the gym biweekly for 2 1/2 hours of strength and stamina training.

Mirek's first dive on the *Carl D. Bradley* was on July 6th, 2001 from the *Pride of Michigan* under the command of Captain Luke Clyburn. This dive was almost over before it began.

Mirek's story:

The plan called for using a small boat, the *Explorer*, and side scan sonar to find the wreck. Fortunately the numbers, given to me by Jim & Pat Stayer, were correct and we were able to locate the wreck in approximately 15 minutes.

It took me almost two hours to set up my support divers and my equipment. At this time the seas were picking up and the waves were approaching three to four feet. At 7:15 PM we started to transfer my support divers and their equipment, using a small inflatable boat, from the *Pride of Michigan* to the *Explorer*, which was anchored to the wreck.

Mirek Standowicz aboard the *Pride of Michigan*
Photo Credit--Luke Clyburn

It took me another 45 minutes to set up my equipment and jump from the *Pride of Michigan*. With the inflatable, they towed me to the *Explorer,* where I had to attach two more tanks and grab my video camera.

I started my descent all the way down to 348 feet. It took me 10 minutes to get to the unloading boom. Unfortunately, when I looked to my left and then I looked to my right, I had no idea which way to go to the pilothouse. At this point I decide to go down to the cargo hold and see what was there. I was starting to go down when I saw my ascent line was trapped between two sharp metal objects. I quickly decided to abort my dive and start my ascent to the surface. At 315 feet my ascent line broke. I heard a deep boom and I knew I was in trouble. I would have to make a free ascent, which is not an easy task in total darkness with seven tanks plus a video

161

camera. Despite my troubles I was most worried about my support divers, because it is easier to find one missing diver on Lake Michigan than three.

Around 30 feet I look up, and it was as if I had seen an angel, it was Terry. She had come to me with extra gases. It was a beautiful moment, because at that point I knew that nothing had happened to them and everything would be ok. When I finally surfaced it was dark and I had drifted nearly a mile from the wreck site.

After the dive was over, I was very happy because I was the first diver to visit the *Carl D. Bradley*, and happier that everyone was ok. I knew I had to go back and I also knew I had to do the next dive a little bit differently.

*   *   *

About a week after his first dive on the *Bradley* Mirek called Jim & Pat Stayer of Lakeshore Charters. The Stayers own a dive charter business and operate a 28-foot catamaran that is specially equipped for deep diving operations. Mirek explained what he wanted to do, and the Stayers agreed to help. While Mirek would be responsible for planning the actual dive, the Stayers would handle everything else. Bob Geno was enlisted to help crew the boat while Tim Juhl provide air cover with his Cessna 182, allowing them to locate Mirek in the event that he was forced to make another free ascent.

The team gathered at Manistique Harbor on the morning of August 6th, 2001, and prepared their equipment for the dive to the *Bradley*. This time the plan was to use heavier rope, terminated by a custom made grapple at the end of 15 feet of chain. Jim explained that the extra weight was needed to sink the thicker polypropylene rope quickly.

Mirek Standowicz - the first man to dive the *Carl D. Bradley*

The wind was increasing and the weather forecast was doubtful, so Jim and Mirek took a quick trip out of the harbor to check lake conditions. The waves were starting to build so the decision was made to postpone the attempt for a day. A slip was rented in the Marina and the *Wildkat* secured for the night.

Tuesday morning dawned bright and clear, with a forecast of diminishing winds all day. The water in the harbor was like glass, and only gentle swells greeted the *Wildkat* as she made her way onto Lake Michigan. Navigating by GPS, the 23-mile trip to the *Bradley's* final resting place was uneventful except for the rising excitement felt by those on board.

The *Bradley* lies in 370 feet of water approximately six miles southwest of Boulder Reef. Arriving at her coordinates, it took about 30 minutes of circling the site to locate what they felt would be the *Bradley's* pilothouse area. A light line tied to a mushroom anchor was dropped over the wreck. Its attached float would be used as a reference point while the *Wildkat* moved upwind to prepare the mooring line. The idea was that the team dropped the grapple and mooring line upwind of the *Bradley* and then drift back into the wreck.

To make such a deep dive required an incredible amount of equipment. Fully suited, Mirek's gear weighed over 200 pounds. In all, Mirek wore 7 tanks filled with different gas mixes needed to sustain him at the *Bradley's* great depth. Mirek carefully calculated all the decompression stops for his dive and wrote the information on a card worn on his arm. To avoid getting the "bends" Mirek had to spend a total of 98 minutes decompressing at different depths. His last stop, at 10 feet below the surface, was for 39 minutes. The plan called for his safety divers, Terry and Natalie to meet Mirek at 90 feet with extra scuba tanks in case he needed them.

Mirek begins his descent to the *Carl D. Bradley*
Photo Credit--Pat Stayer

After he entered the water and his tanks were secure, he took his video camera. At the line, Mirek gave his equipment one more check and then began his long descent to the wreck. As he disappeared into the depths Mirek appeared to be literally surrounded by scuba tanks.

Safely back aboard the Wildkat, *Mirek describes his dive on the Carl D. Bradley:*

Two minutes after leaving the surface I was able to see the *Carl D. Bradley*. It was overwhelming. What I realized right away was that I was on the bow, and I couldn't believe how everything was in such excellent shape. You could see the white and red paint, and there was just a little bit of silt here and there.

The pilothouse of the *Carl D. Bradley*
Photo Credit--Mirek Standowicz

The Stayers dropped me exactly on the pilothouse...I turned a little to my left and I could see that the pilothouse was coming. Woo!!!...So I just turned around. There is a LOT OF CURRENT. I had a hard time stopping with all my tanks. I landed where there were cabins, on the lower levels. So I said to myself, the pilothouse has to be above. I swam to the bow and started up to the pilothouse. This was my point of destination. At that moment my heart started to beat rapidly as the beam of my lights started to slide up toward the pilothouse. Soon I was able to see the name, *Carl D. Bradley*. It was a fantastic feeling, unbelievable. I will never be able to forget that. It was a big moment for me. Looking at the ship I had an overwhelming feeling that was like walking through a ghost town that used to be full of life.

I approached one of the windows. The glass was blown out and there were some sharp edges. I squeezed in and shot some video. Then I moved down a couple windows and shot some more. Looking into the window I could see the telegraph. It was in the vertical, or stop, position. Next to it was the helm and the ship's wheel. Everything seemed to be in perfect shape, except the broken windows. I swam up to the top of the pilothouse to the searchlight. It too was in excellent condition.

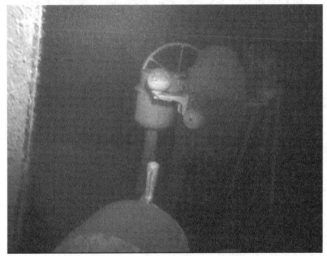

Inside the pilothouse of the *Carl D. Bradley*
Photo Credit--Mirek Standowicz

Unfortunately time was running out. I had to find my ascent line. As I looked down I could make out the bow of the ship, the visibility was very good. It is unbelievable how dark it is at 320 feet. No matter how I looked up down, to the left to the right it is pitch black. It is really spooky. On the other hand it seems like the *Bradley* is standing proudly on the bottom, ready to sail. It was time for me to prepare myself for the accent to the surface and this was an awfully long way from 321 feet in total darkness.

The second dive was completely different when compared to my first dive. It was as though this time the *Bradley* accepted my presence and allowed me to put on video tape her beauty, because that is the best way to describe her. She is beautiful!

When people ask me, "Why the *Carl D. Bradley?*" My answer is very simple. I did it because nobody had done it before and I wanted to be the first.

An artist's conception of the *Bradley* as it rests
on the bottom of Lake Michigan

©Robert McGreevy

Appendix C.

Voices from the *Sundew's* Crew

Captain Harold Muth

Captain Harold D. Muth, USCG Ret., was born in St. Joseph, Michigan on April 1, 1921. He enlisted in the United States Coast Guard at Chicago, Illinois in February 1941. Upon completion of recruit training he began his Coast Guard career as an apprentice seaman. Muth rose quickly through the enlisted ranks and was sent to Officers Candidate School where he received his commission. He served in both the Atlantic and Pacific Theaters during WWII, mostly on convoy duty. While aboard the USCG Patrol Cutter *Triton*, he took part in the sinking of two German U Boats. As gunnery officer of the Destroyer Escort *USS Howard D. Crow* DE—252, he escorted 22 convoys between the U.S. and Europe. Following the end of hostilities in Europe, Muth accompanied the *Crow* to the Pacific, where he was when the A-Bombs were dropped on Japan. Muth returned to the U.S. west coast in 1946 and was Acting Commanding Officer of the *Crow* at the time of its decommissioning.

His first command after WWII was a Loran Station on St. Paul Island in the middle of the Bering Sea. His next command was an ex—Lighthouse Service buoy tender, based in Ketchikan Alaska, the USCGC *Hemlock*. Upon completion of three years servicing aids-to-navigation in southeast Alaska, and a total of five years plus of Alaskan duty he headed for the warmer climes of southern California, much to the delight of his family. In the spring of 1957 Muth was given command of the USCGC *Sundew*, based in Sturgeon Bay, Wisconsin, and later at Charlevoix, Michigan. His next, and last command at sea, was the USCGC *Chilula*, operating out of Morehead City, North Carolina.

His final assignment was Chief of Staff at the 2nd Coast Guard District Headquarters in St. Louis, MO, where he retired in 1975 after 34 1/2 years on active duty.

He and Doloras, his wife of more than 60 years, currently reside in Bradenton, Florida. They have four children, seven grandchildren and one great-grandchild.

Warren Toussaint

Hospital Corpsman Warren Toussaint was born on February 17, 1926, in Milwaukee, Wisconsin. While serving in the U.S. Navy in WWII, he trained as a Corpsman and was slated to go overseas with the Marines when the A-bomb changed everything. On the day that he graduated from Marquette University, he heard the news that North Korea had attacked South Korea. A member of the Naval Reserve, Warren was called to active duty in August 1950. He hurriedly married his sweetheart Norma, and after three months of additional training he was ordered to Japan.  While overseas, he served on a Navy Surgical Medical Team and made four trips to Korea where he had what he modestly describes as some "tough moments." Warren returned home in January 1951, and was finally able to see his first born child who had just turned eight months old.

Changing services, Warren joined the Coast Guard and served on the cutters *Kukui, Sundew, Mackinaw,* and *Glacier*. He even served five months in Antarctica aboard a CG ice breaker. His most memorable experience while in the Coast Guard was the search and rescue efforts that followed the sinking of the *Carl D. Bradley*.

Warren Toussaint retired from U.S. Coast Guard 1981 after 33 years of active duty (including his Naval service.) After retirement he worked for Blue Cross / Shield of California and Blue Cross of South Carolina.

Toussaint currently resides in Oshkosh, Wisconsin. He has been happily married for 53 years and has three grown children. He is active in the American Legion and his favorite hobbies are reading, history, and public speaking.

Robert Fitz

Damage Controlman Robert J. Fitz was born on May 19, 1932, and grew up on his parents' dairy farm west of Sandusky, Ohio. He worked on the farm until the age of 23, when he received his Draft notice. Not wanting to go into the army, he chose to enlist in the U.S. Coast Guard. Fitz's choice of services was based upon his desire to help save lives, not take them.

After four years of service in the Coast Guard, Robert worked briefly for General Motors before taking a job with the Ford Motor Company. When the GI Bill was reinstated, Robert went to college at Bowling Green University while still working full time at the John C. Opfeo Excavating Company. Graduating with a degree in Elementary Education, Robert went on to get his Masters while teaching full time. In his 24 year education career, he taught third, fifth, and sixth grade.

Robert and his wife Mary Ann have two children, Robert and David. The couple enjoys traveling in Michigan's Upper Peninsula.

Appendix D.

A History of the Bradley Transportation Company and the *SS Carl D. Bradley*

I. The Rogers City Connection:

Located on the shore of Lake Huron in the northern part of Michigan's lower peninsula, Rogers City began life as a small fishing village. In the late 1800's during the rush to harvest Michigan's white pine, Rogers City grew along with the timber trade. Northern Michigan was dotted with lumber camps during these years, with the majority of timber being shipped out aboard Great Lakes vessels. As the trees were cleared, it became obvious that there was a large limestone

A "lumber train" in early Rogers City
Photo credit--ML Screenings

outcropping south of Rogers City near a small village known as Crawford's Quarry. Although it was the first settlement in the area, by the early 1900's Crawford's Quarry was little more than a ghost town.

In 1907 & 1908, geologists visited the area and surveyed the extent of the limestone deposit. Based upon their reports, the Michigan Limestone and Chemical Company was established in 1910, buying 8000 acres to begin developing

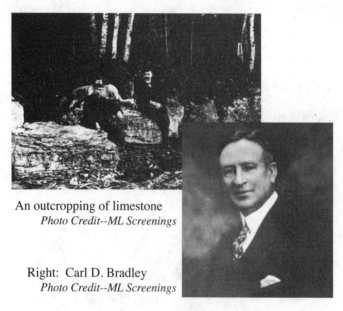

An outcropping of limestone
Photo Credit--ML Screenings

Right: Carl D. Bradley
Photo Credit--ML Screenings

what would one day become the largest limestone quarry in the world. As America became more and more industrialized, the demand for products derived from limestone increased. A wide range of uses including steel making, cement, chemicals, glass and agricultural fertilizer required limestone, so the company's future looked promising.

In 1911, Carl D. Bradley moved from Chicago to Rogers City to become the company's third managing director. Those who knew Carl Bradley described him as a charming and engaging man, who worked tirelessly to advance the interests of his company.

Early on he realized that if the company was to grow and be successful, it must have a reliable means of delivering limestone to its markets. He envisioned a fleet of self unloading vessels that could carry limestone into even the most rudimentary ports, unloading their cargo without the need of dockside equipment.

II. The Bradley Transportation Company and the

Carl D. Bradley:

The first ship to join what would be known as the Bradley Transportation Company was the 436 foot *Calcite*, built in 1912. The *W.F. White* was the second ship added to the fleet. She was built in 1915. The third ship to join the fleet was first vessel to carry the name *Carl D. Bradley*.

Construction on the hull of the *Carl D. Bradley*
Photo Credit--ML Screenings

In 1927, when the *Carl D. Bradley* that we know was built, the first *Bradley* was renamed the *John G. Munson*. In 1952 it was renamed for a third time, becoming the *Irvin L. Clymer*. It carried that name until being scrapped in 1994. The second *Carl D. Bradley* was built by the American Shipbuilding

Company in Lorain, Ohio. She measured 638 feet long, 65 feet wide with a depth of 33 feet. Like the other vessels of the Bradley fleet, she was of a self-unloading design.

Her hull was built in the form of a double hopper, with conveyer belts passing below. The conveyors carried the limestone forward to a bucket mechanism that raised it up to a 165 foot unloading boom located on the spar deck just behind the forward deckhouse. The boom could be swung out over the side to unload the cargo where needed.

The *Bradley's* engines were of an interesting design, in which high pressure boilers were used to provide steam to an turbine-driven electric generator. The generator in turn powered an electric motor which drove the ship's propeller. This combination produced up to 5000 shaft horsepower and could drive the fully-loaded *Bradley* at speeds of up to 14 MPH.

Launched on April 9th, 1927, the *Bradley* completed her outfitting and then sailed to Rogers City where she joined the rest of the Bradley Fleet on July 28th. With all her flags flying, the *Carl D. Bradley* steamed into port for the first time. She was met by the tug *Rogers City* with Mrs. Bradley and the town's band aboard. Operations at the calcite plant were suspended for several hours that morning, and hundreds of employees and townspeople gathered to witness the arrival of the huge vessel.

After a welcoming speech by the village president, Carl D. Bradley himself spoke to the crowd, praising the ship, her crew and the men who built her. At that time, the *Bradley* was the largest vessel on the Great Lakes. Her first trip carrying stone for the company was to Buffington, near Gary, Indiana. Ironically, it would be on a return trip from Gary 31 years later that the *Bradley* was lost. In 1929 she hauled a record 18,113 tons of limestone on a single trip, a record for lake vessels that would stand until 1942. Unfortunately, Mr. Bradley was not able to savor this accomplishment, having died in California in March of the previous year.

For the most part the years passed uneventfully for the *Carl D. Bradley* as she hauled limestone to ports throughout the Great Lakes. A few events do bear mentioning, however. In the fall of 1939, local papers carried reports of her exploits in rescuing the crew of the stricken tugboat *Badger State*. The tug's engines had failed, and her crew had fired off flares to get the attention of the passing *Bradley*, which took the tug in tow. Unfortunately, a wave swamped the tug, casting her crew into the frigid lake. The *Bradley* picked up the tug's three crewmen, but the tug's captain died a short time later of exposure.

During the winter layup of 1940, the *Bradley* had a new rudder and prop installed. Of one-piece magnesium-bronze construction, this propeller would maintain its polish and thus its speed longer than conventional propellers which had individual blades bolted to a hub. The design also resulted in a smooth flow of water over the rudder which produced excellent handling characteristics.

On July 11th, 1943, the $14 million MacArthur Lock opened at the Soo. The *Carl D. Bradley* claimed the honor of being the first ship to "lock-thru." The following year, the *Bradley* had her unloading boom lengthened 40 feet, bringing its total length to 205 feet. At same time, the "A" frame and deck were strengthened to support the stress imposed by the longer boom.

In 1947 the *Bradley* received its first radar. Originally developed during WWII to warn of enemy planes, the addition

176

The *Carl D. Bradley* was the first boat through the MacArthur Lock
Photo Credit--ML Screenings

of radar helped the *Bradley* and other ships to navigate safely during periods of poor visibility.

During the winter layup of 1947 the steel parts that supported the conveyor belts were replaced. A new type welder was used that allowed the job to be done seven times faster than would have been the case if it had been done manually. On April 3, 1956, the *Bradley* was involved in a collision with the Canadian Motor Vessel *White Rose*. The *Bradley* sustained minor damage below the waterline on the starboard side, in the vicinity of the number 10 hatch. By coincidence, the *Bradley* broke apart near this same area.

During winter layup prior to the 1958 season, missing rivets were found in the hold that were replaced with 3/4 inch carriage bolts. This was a bit of a departure from the normal procedure, but was approved by the Coast Guard.

177

In March of 1958, the Bradley Transportation set a world record for being the first marine transportation company to go 1000 days without any employee suffering a disabling injury. This record would end at 1303 days with the loss of the *Carl D. Bradley*.

The Bradley Transportation Company celebrates a world record
Photo Credit--ML Screenings

In May of 1958, the *Bradley* struck bottom in the harbor at Cedarville, causing minor damage. This, and another grounding in November, which fractured a hull plate beneath the engine room, were never reported to the Coast Guard.

Business was slow in 1958, and the *Bradley* spent the summer months in layup. In October, the *Bradley* was returned to service, back in her old role of hauling limestone. The limestone trade was hard on ships. As a result, the *Bradley* was scheduled to go to Manitowoc, Wisconsin at the end of the shipping season to have extensive repairs to her cargo area and to have a centerline bulkhead installed. It was hoped that this bulkhead would increase the longitudinal strength of the *Bradley* by a moderate amount.

On November 16th, in the early hours of Sunday morning, the *Carl D. Bradley* eased into the harbor at Cedarville, Michigan, to take on a load of Dolomite consigned to Gary, Indiana. As she steamed down Lake Michigan, a huge storm which had developed in the southwest was just beginning to make its presence felt. Rising winds resulted in small craft warnings being issued for Lake Michigan, but the *Bradley* made the trip to Gary with little trouble. She was lost in a gale on November 18th, while attempting to return to her home port of Rogers City, Michigan.

Thirty-three of her thirty-five man crew were lost in the sinking.

Appendix E.
Results of the USCG Inquiry
(CARL D. BRADLEY A-9 Bd)

7 JULY 1959

Commandant's Action

on

Marine Board of Investigation; foundering of the
SS CARL D. BRADLEY, Lake Michigan,
18 November 1958 with loss of life

1. The record of the Marine Board of Investigation convened
to investigate subject casualty together with its findings of
Fact, Opinions and Recommendations has been reviewed

2. The SS CARL D. BRADLEY Official Number 226776,
a self-unloading bulk freighter of 10,028 gross tons, built in
1927, departed Gary, Indiana, on 17 November 1958 en route
to Calcite, Michigan, in ballast. At the time of departure
the wind was 25 - 35 MPH from the south and the weather
forecast was for whole gale winds, 50 to 65 MPH from the
south shifting to the southwest. The BRADLEY proceeded
up the Wisconsin shore at distances off varying from 5 to 12
miles. Although the wind velocity increased during the period,
sea conditions were not considered severe and the vessel
was riding smoothly. Sometime early in the afternoon of 18
November in the vicinity of Cana Island course was altered
to 046 degrees True to cross Lake Michigan toward Lansing
Shoal. While proceeding on this course the wind reached a
velocity of 60 to 65 MPH from the southwest. The speed of
the vessel was between 14 and 15 knots. The seas were slightly
on the starboard quarter and according to the Chief Mate, who
was on watch at the time of the casualty and was one of the two

survivors, the seas were estimated to be 20 feet in height with 50 to 75 feet between the crests. The vessel continued to ride smoothly, however, both as to roll and to pitch. At 1730 just at dusk while still on course 046 a noise described as a thud followed by a vibration was heard. The Chief Mate looked aft and saw the stern of the vessel sagging and it was immediately realized that the vessel was in serious trouble. The general alarm was sounded and the crew prepared to abandon ship. Distress calls on the radio-telephone were made by the Chief Mate who gave the vessel's position as 12 miles southwest of Gull Island Light. These calls were received by several radio stations, both commercial and Coast Guard. Within two or three minutes the BRADLEY heaved upward near No. 10 hatch, which is approximately amidships, and broke in two. The bow settled from aft, then rolled over and sank. The liferaft stowed forward which was being readied floated free. The stern settled from forward then plunged with a flash of flame and smoke as the water reached the boiler room. Four crew members managed to board the liferaft immediately after the casualty but two were lost during the night.

3. A German cargo vessel, the M/V CHRISTIAN SARTORI was approximately four miles from the BRADLEY at the time of the casualty and observed the flash of flame from which she concluded the BRADLEY had exploded. Course was immediately altered for the scene but due to the adverse sea conditions she did not arrive at the estimated position of the sinking until approximately one and one-half hours later.

4. Coast Guard air and surface units, assisted by the SARTORI until 0200, 19 November, searched the area throughout the night with the aircraft providing flare illumination. Weather conditions and darkness severely handicapped the search and it was not until 0825, 19 November that the raft carrying the

181

only two survivors was located. After daybreak eight other merchant vessels joined the search. Later in the morning the lifeboat from the after end of the BRADLEY was located in an overturned condition. Of the thirty-five persons reported to have been aboard the BRADLEY there were, in addition to the two survivors, eighteen bodies recovered. Fifteen are still missing and are presumed dead. At the present time efforts to locate and identify the wreck of the BRADLEY are still continuing.

REMARKS

1. Concurring with the Board, it is considered that the BRADLEY did not strike Boulder Reef but rather that she broke in two and the eruption of steam and combustible materials as she went down gave rise to the mistaken assumption on the part of the CHRISTIAN SARTORI witnesses that the vessel exploded.

2. Although in all probability the vessel broke in hogging, the implication in the Board's conclusion that the fracture resulted because the vessel encountered an unusual wave condition while in ballast is not supported in the record. In the absence of any evidence of improper or unusual ballasting such reasoning would necessarily require an assumption that the waves were unique in the vessel's twenty-one* year history of navigation in the Great Lakes. This premise and the conclusion must therefore be rejected, particularly in view of the survivors description or how smoothly the vessel was riding, a point of which the Board took special note and which was further supported by the statement of the Second Mate of the SS JOHNSTOWN. For this reason the Board's conclusion that the Master of the BRADLEY exercised poor judgment in proceeding across northern Lake Michigan from Cana Island

toward Lansing Shoal is also disapproved.
The Carl D. Bradley had been sailing for 31 years, not 21.

3. The Board has offered no other conclusions as to the possible cause of this disaster and an exhaustive review of the record has likewise failed to yield any positive determinations in this regard. Contrary to the Board's opinions, however, the following factors may have had some causal connection and cannot be discounted merely for the lack of probative evidence:

a. The unexplained presence of the hairline cracks discovered in the vessel's underbody amidships during drydocking in Chicago in May 1957 strongly suggest the possibility of structural weakness.

b. The two unreported groundings experienced by the BRADLEY in the spring of 1958 and November of 1958 may have introduced unusual hull stresses. It is because such possibilities exist that 116 CFR 136.05-1 requires a Notice of Marine Casualty to be filed with the Coast Guard in all cases of stranding or grounding whether or not there is apparent damage.

c. The extensive renewal of cargo hold side slopes, screen bulkheads and tank tops planned by the company for the 1958-1959 winter lay-up is in itself indicative of wear and deterioration and raises the obvious question as to the general condition of the vessel's structure.

The possibilities raised by the foregoing coupled with the fact that the vessel broke up and foundered under conditions which, while severe, she should easily have been able to weather, leads inevitably to the conclusion that the vessel had developed an undetected structural weakness or defect. Due to the significance of such a possibility, particularly with respect to other vessels of similar design and vintage, consideration will be given to the initiation of an underwater survey of the BRADLEY depending, of course, on when and where the vessel is ultimately located and any other practical aspects which might limit the benefits to be derived from such examination.

4. Regardless of any other determinations, this casualty has emphasized the need for the program of technical evaluation to determine if there is any evidence of structural defects in other vessels of the Great Lakes fleet. Such a program has been initiated. In addition, a reappraisal of present inspection procedures as applied to Great Lakes vessels is indicated looking toward the adoption of such standards and methods that will increase the likelihood of early detection of possible structural weaknesses particularly in the case of the older vessels. The Commander, Ninth Coast Guard District has been directed to make such a study with due regard for the peculiarities and problems attendant to the seasonal operation of Great Lakes vessels. In the course of such study the Commander, Ninth Coast Guard District has been directed to adopt any reasonable procedure within the framework of present laws and regulations and to make further recommendations for any legislative or regulatory changes which appear necessary. Finally, it is considered that this casualty has dictated a need for owners and operators to re examine their responsibilities to establish and maintain safe operating and maintenance standards.

5. The Board's recommendations concerning lifejacket crotch straps, an additional liferaft, lifeboat mechanical disengaging apparatus, lifeboat painters and parachute type distress signals

merit further consideration and will be made the subject of study by the Merchant Marine Council.

6. Subject to the foregoing remarks, the record of the Marine Board of Investigation is approved.

A. C. Richmond
Vice Admiral, U.S. Coast Guard
Commandant

Appendix F.
USCG Finding of Fact in the Loss of the *Carl D. Bradley*

After full and mature deliberation, the board finds as follows:

<u>Findings Of Fact</u>

1. The particulars on SS CARL D. BRADLEY:

Name:	Carl D. Bradley
Owner:	Michigan Limestone Division, U.S. Steel Corporation
Official No:	226776
Tonnage:	10028 Gross; 7706 Net
Home Port:	New York
Type Vessel:	Self-unloading bulk freighter
Dimensions:	623'x 65'x 33'
Propulsion:	Steam, single screw, turbo-electrical, two Foster-Wheeler boilers 450#
Classification	Lloyd's Register of Shipping, 1OOA1 and LMC
Builder:	American Shipbuilding Company, Lorain, Ohio, yard, 1927, hull number 797
Master:	Roland Bryan, Loudonville, New York
Chief Engineer:	Raymond Buehler, 1500 Cordova Avenue, Lakewood, Ohio

2. The CARL D. BRADLEY was given her last annual inspection at Calcite, Michigan, by Commander Mark L. Hocking and Lieutenant Frank M. Sperry, inspectors from the OCMI Office, St. Ignace, Michigan. This inspection started

on 30 January 1958 and was completed on 17 April 1958, and a certificate of inspection was issued on that date.

3. The CARL D. BRADLEY had an established load line. The current certificate issued by Lloyd's Register of Shipping was last endorsed on 26 February 1958 by Mr. J. D. Wallace and R. S. Haugenson, surveyor.

4. During the 1957-58-winter lay-up, miscellaneous cargo hold repairs were effected. These included the replacement of deteriorated and loose rivets by carriage bolts in the hopper side slope plates. Although the Coast Guard had not given prior approval to these repairs, they were considered adequate by Lieutenant Sperry when he viewed the work in progress. These repairs were later reported by the Master to be holding satisfactorily, and there was no report of leaking in the side tanks during the 1958 season.

5. The CARL D. BRADLEY was scheduled for extensive cargo hold renewal and replacement during the 1958-59-winter lay-up. This work was to be performed at Manitowoc Shipbuilding Company, Manitowoc, Wisconsin, and was to consist primarily of the reconstruction of the tank top, renewal of the cargo hold side slopes and screen bulkheads, and the installation of a centerline bulkhead between frames 32 and 70 as shown on H.C. Downer and Associates Drawings YD 411-S9-3-1 (Appendix "Y") and YD 411-S11-11-1 (Appendix "Z") approved by the Coast Guard on 25 February 1958 and by Lloyd's on 11 October 1957. A comparison of the midship section, as originally built (Exhibit 6), and that shown on H.C. Downer Drawing YD-41 1-S11-11-1 (Appendix "Z" indicates that the above work would have increased the longitudinal strength by a moderate amount. It was also the owner's intent to dry-dock the vessel in Chicago after the completion of the work in Manitowoc for its five-year survey, the last five-year

survey docking having been accomplished in Lorain, Ohio, in 1953.

6. The CARL D. BRADLEY was in drydock for period 9-15 May 1957 Chicago, Illinois, to effect repairs incident to damages sustained on 3 April 1956 in a collision with M/V WHITE ROSE at South East Bend, St. Clair River. These repairs consisted of inserting one (1) new bilge plate 21 feet long to replace damaged sections of Plates E-14 and E-15 starboard, and minor fairing and riveting to shell plates K-8 and K-9 port side. In addition, hairline fractures in the transverse direction, location for the most part at the after edge of the riveted lap butts, were found in bottom plates B-16, D-16, D-16, D-19 starboard, and B-14, B-1 5, C-9, C-1 6, and D-12 port. These plates were repaired by cropping out the fractured sections repaired these plates and the adjacent riveted lap butts and inserting a new full-width section approximately six feet in length. In effecting these repairs, the butts were flush welded and the seams were riveted. Satisfactory temporary repairs were also made to shell plate J-20 aft on the port side in way of the engine room forward bulkhead and internals in way of this plate and miscellaneous repairs were also made on the starboard side aft, exact location unknown.

7. On two known occasions between the drydocking in May 1957 and the casualty, the CARL. D. BRADLEY sustained bottom damage. In the spring of *1958*, the vessel rubbed bottom while proceeding out of Cedarville, Michigan, and damage was incurred just aft of the collision bulkhead in way of No: 1 water bottom, port. The owners considered this damage to be such of minor extent that no repairs were necessary. In early November 1958, the vessel again rubbed bottom while port, in the A and B strakes. This damage, a transverse fracture approximately 14" long, was repaired

afloat at Calcite, Michigan, by the owners' repair force by welding a channel bar over the fracture and blanking each end to form a coffer dam. The size of this channel is not known.

8. Neither of the above-mentioned damages were reported to the Coast Guard or Lloyd's and the repair in No. 7 water bottoms was neither reported to nor approved by the Coast Guard.

9. On 30 October 1958, a safety inspection was conducted on board the CARL D. BRADLEY by Lieutenant Sperry, This inspection consisted of a fire drill and a boat drill, during which both boats were swung out and No: 2 boat was lowered into the water and 28 crewmen exercised under oars to the satisfaction of the inspector. It was during this visit to the vessel that the Master reported that the repairs to the side tanks were holding up satisfactorily.

10. The CARL. D. BRADLEY was of typical arrangement of self-unloading type vessel with a forepeak and large cargo area, and having propulsion machinery aft. These areas were separated by two transverse watertight bulkheads, the collision bulkhead at frame 12 and the engine room forward bulkhead frame 173. The cargo hold space was divided into five compartments by screen bulkheads above the tunnel and the unloading machinery was located in the conveyor room just forward of the cargo spaces. The entire 475 foot length of the cargo spaces was open longitudinally thought the tunnel and conveyor room.

11. The CARL D. BRADLEY was engaged in the limestone and coal trade, operating primarily between the limestone ports on Lake Huron and unloading ports on Lake Michigan and Lake Erie. The 1958 season began on 22 April and the CARL D. BRADLEY had completed 43 round trips before the casualty. The vessel was not in operation for a

period of about three months commencing about 1 July and ending about 1 October by reason of business lag. During this period,. The vessel lay at Calcite, Michigan, with only a watchman on board.

12. Captain Bryan had been sailing as Master of the CARL. D. BRADLEY since 1954. Chief Engineer Bueler had served on the CARL D. BRADLEY for almost the entire life of the vessel and as Chief Engineer since 1952.

13. The manager of the Bradley Transportation fleet is Mr. Norman Hoeft and he has held his present position for approximately two years. He has had no sailing experience, but had been in the employment of Michigan Limestone Division for some 33 years in various capacities. His last previous assignment was in the traffic department.

14. Present management knew of no company instructions issued concerning the sequence of loading, unloading or ballasting of their vessels. They consider that the responsibility in these matters is vested in the ships' masters. There were certain practices followed on the CARL D. BRADLEY which developed into recommended procedures as a result of the experience of vessel personnel and which was passed on by masters and mates to their successors.

15. The Master and Chief Engineer of the CARL D. BRADLEY were charged with the responsibility of keeping the management advised as to the repairs, maintenance and upkeep requirements. The management structure of the Bradley Fleet, which consisted of nine vessels, did not provide for a fleet captain or a fleet engineer.

16. The safety directors of the Bradley Transportation fleet had not, in his four (4) years in his present capacity, received any complaints of unsafe or hazardous operating conditions on

190

the CARL D. BRADLEY. It is noted that the safety program, as administered by the safety directors for the Bradley fleet, was almost solely devoted to industrial-type safety conditions and did not encompass vessel material conditions. For success in this field, the National Safety Council presented an award of honor to the Bradley Transportation Line, Michigan Limestone Division, Rogers City Michigan, for the world's record in having 2,228,755 injury-free man-hours, 24 April 1955 to 31 December 1957. The present safety director had not at any time personally made a material condition inspection on the CARL D. BRADLEY.

17. The CARL D. BRADLEY departed Gary, Indiana, bound for Calcite, Michigan at approximately 2200 on 17 November 1958. Prior to departure, the Master and Mate had knowledge of the weather forecast, which at 2000 warned of whole gale winds (50-65 MPH) from the south, shifting to southwest, at the time of departure, the wind was fresh (25-35 MPH) from the south and there was no sea.

18. When the CARL D. BRADLEY was secured for sea, special attention was given to the hatch clamps and boom stays, because of the impending weather. The vessel was in a light condition with the forward tanks only partially ballasted. The ballasting of the after tanks (5,6 and 7 and Trim) was handled by the engineering force, and the amount of water in the after tanks during this voyage could not be determined. However, normal practice was to have the vessel ballasted full aft to get the propeller down, and the vessel would, therefore, have had a draft between 17'6" and 18' aft. The forward draft was not measured at the time of departure, The above was the normal ballasting procedure for departing port without cargo.

19. At 0400 on 18 November 1958, the CARL D. BRADLEY passed Milwaukee at a distance of 11 miles,

making approximately 15 MPH, and was abeam Sheboygan at 0700, a distance of seven miles. Two lake freighters, SS GOVENOR MILLER and RICHARD TREMBEL, were running parallel with the CARL D. BRADLEY and closer to shore. The wind increased steadily after 0400, and during the 4-8 watch, the water ballast was increased to the maximum practical condition of 10, 16, 18, and 18 feet in tanks #1, 2, 3, and 4 respectively. The vessel remain ballasted in this manner until the casualty.

20. The CARL D. BRADLEY continued up to the Wisconsin Shore at distances off varying from five to 12 miles. From a point off Cana Island, a course of 046 true was set across Northern Lake Michigan toward a point midway between Seul Choix Point and Lansing Shoal. Sometime prior to 1600 speed had been reduced by about 10 RPM so that the vessel was making approximately 14-15 MPH. At 1519 a fix was plotted by the Second Mate from visual bearings, and this position indicated the vessel to be slightly to the south of the line drawn on the chart for the route across Lake Michigan.

21. At 1600, when First Mate Elmer Fleming came on watch, the master was on the bridge and in charge of the navigation. The CARL D. BRADLEY was past Poverty Island on course 046 true and was riding comfortably with a heavy following sea slightly on the starboard quarter, The wind had increased to whole gale force (60-65 MPH) and shifted to southwest.

22. The SS JOHNSON, ahead of the CARL D. BRADLEY by several hours, passed Boulder Reef at about 1317, and had reported encountering a very heavy sea there at that time. The only other lake freighter which reported passing Boulder Reef, was the SS CHARLES L. HUTCHINSON, which passed the reef at 0554 on the 18th, downbound and

loaded. This vessel reduced speed at 0700, because of heavy seas. All other lake vessel that reported having been in the northern Lake Michigan area at this time reported that they had sought shelter, and at least eight vessels were anchored or proceeding to anchor at the time of the casualty, either in Green Bay, at Garden Island, or in the Straits of Mackinac.

23. Sometime after 1600 the radar was placed in operation and was used for all subsequent navigation, except for a RDF bearing of 051 true obtained on Lansing Shoal sometime before 1700. After the fix obtained at 1519 was plotted on the chart, no later positions were plotted. However, radar observations indicated that on the course being steered (046° true), the vessel would clear Boulder Reef and Gull Island by at least five miles. At about 1720, radar ranges were taken on the north end of South Fox Island and on Point aux Barques, which again showed the vessel to be slightly to the right of the course line drawn on the chart.

24. Within one-half hour before the casualty, both survivors, Fleming and Mays, had occasion to traverse on length of the vessel from the forward house to the after house on the weather deck, and neither one saw nor heard anything out of the ordinary which would have caused them to be concerned with the safety of the vessel. In addition, Mays also went aft to the engine room and returned to the fore part of the vessel through the tunnel, and again, neither saw nor heard anything unusual. Up to the time of the casualty the vessel was riding easily, taking no water over the deck, and with so smooth a motion that the sideboards were not necessary on the mess table. Accordingly, persons on board were not aware of any reason to be concerned for the safety of the vessel.

25. The bulkhead at the forward end of the engine and boiler spaces, "Blk #173" was fitted with a dogged watertight

door, which opened forward into the tunnel. The door was normally kept closed, although rarely if ever completely dogged. Just prior to the casualty, when Mays was aft to pump the water from the sump at the after end of the tunnel, he used this door, and when last leaving it, tightened at least one dog. The sumping of the water in the tunnel was regularly assigned duty of the deck watch to be performed each watch, and on this occasion Mays found no more than the normal amount of water in the tunnel.

26. At approximately 1730, without warning, a sound described as a thud was heard on the bridge of the CARL D. BRADLEY. The thud, which Fleming could not more adequately describe, was followed by a vibration similar to that which is felt in a vessel pounding into a sea, with the propeller out of water but the thud was such as to cause Fleming to instinctively realize that the vessel was in serious trouble. Looking aft, Fleming noted that the stern of the CARL D. BRADLEY was sagging.

27. After pumping the sump aft, Mays proceeded through the tunnel on the tank top to the conveyor room forward and was there when he also heard the thud, which he was totally unable to describe. However he, too realized that the vessel was in serious trouble and ran immediately for the ladder leading topside. As he departed this compartment, he neither heard nor saw that section of the vessel being flooded.

28. Back on the bridge, the Master immediately sounded the general alarm and began to blow the whistle, while Fleming broadcast "MAY DAY" on channel 51 (2182 kc). This broadcast, which was immediately answered by radio station WAD, Port Washington, Wisconsin, gave the CARL. D. BRADLEY'S position as 12 miles southwest of Gull Island. Upon request by WAD, the CARL D. BRADLEY

verified this position. There had been just enough time to put out two "MAY DAY" messages before the power failed and the lights went out. There were no further signals heard from the CARL D. BRADLEY. The "MAY DAY" was heard and recorded by a large number of stations, including the Coast Guard Lifeboat Station at Charlevoix, Michigan, and primary radio station NMD at Chesterland, Ohio.

29. At 1730, the CARL D. BRADLEY was still on course 046° true, was riding easily and making about 14.5 MPH. The vessel was ballasted to the maximum practical extent with estimated drafts of 13' 9" forward and 17'6" aft. The wind was southwest 55-65 MPH, and the sea was heavy, steep, and about 25 feet high from 1/2 point on the starboard quarter. The approximate air and water temperatures were 40° F and 50° F, respectively. The sun had set at 1710 and there was still 14 minutes of twilight, which would end at 1744.

30. The German M/V CHRISTIAN SARTORI, a 254' general cargo vessel, was at 1730 about four miles distant from the CARL D. BRADLEY, although the CHRISTIAN SARTORI did not hear the "MAY DAY", officers on the bridge witnessed the casualty. The CHRISTIAN SARTORI, southbound, passed Lansing Shoal at 1200. The JOHNSTOWN later reported sighting her at about 1400, one to two miles off her portside, when the JOHNSTOWN was abeam Gull Island light, distance three to four miles on course 050° true. This put the CHRISTIAN SARTORI approximately five miles off Gull Island. At about 1700, the CHRISTIAN SARTORI was on course 215° true making about two MPH when she sighted the CARL D BRADLEY ahead 10-15° on her starboard bow. At 1720, the CHRISTIAN SARTORI came right to course 240° true to pass the CARL D. BRADLEY on her portside, and by 1730 the CHRISTIAN SARTORI was approximately six miles distant from Gull Island, bearing 260° true from

195

Gull Island Light, with the CARL D. BRADLEY 10-15° on her port bow. The only side light of the CARL D. BRADLEY seen at any time by the CHRISTIAN SARTORI was her red light, and at no time was the green side light visible to the CHRISTIAN SARTORI.

31. When the alarm sounded, the crew responded quickly and sought to abandon ship. With the exception of the Second Mate, who tried to go aft toward the boat deck (body not recovered), those forward donned lifejackets and went to the 15-person emergency life raft aft of the pilothouse. Men aft were observed to be on the boat deck and lowering the starboard lifeboat. The two lifeboats were 25-person boats on the boat deck aft and were equipped with quadrantal-type mechanical davits, Manila falls, and common hooks.

32. Two or three minutes after the thud and after the stern had been noted to sag, the vessel heaved upward near hatch #10 and broke in two resulting in two sections approximately 300' in length, 65' wide and 90' high, including the deck houses and superstructure. As the sections parted, the forward end of the stern section, with the lights still on, swung to port and the bow section swung to starboard. The bow section, maintaining an even keel, settled from the after end until the spar (weather) deck was completely submerged, then listed to port, rolled over, and sank. The life raft floated free.

33. The stern section settled from the forward end on an even keel and then plunged, still on an even keel, with the counter going down last. The starboard lifeboat swung forward on its falls. Whether the boat was completely launched before the sinking could not be determined. When recovered, it was upside down, and there was no evidence that it had been occupied. As the section plunged, there was a sudden eruption of steam, bright flame, and smoke.

34. The first indication of anything unusual about the CARL D. BRADLEY, as noticed by the CHRISTIAN SARTORI, was about 1730 when the lights in the forward end were observed to go out. This was followed several minutes later by an explosion with considerable illumination and heavy smoke. When the smoke cleared, the CARL D. BRADLEY had disappeared from view and, whereas they had been getting a good image on the radar, there now was none. The CHRISTIAN SARTORI changed course to 195° true and headed toward the CARL D. BRADLEY'S position and began to search for survivors, which lasted until relieved at 0200, 19 November. Searching proved negative. Approximately one hour after the casualty, the CHRISTIAN SARTORI sighted flares on the water about one mile off her port between the ship and Boulder Reef Buoy and in line with the buoy.

35. The following Coast Guard units participated in the SAR emergency:

a.   Plum Island Lifeboat Station-Heard "MAY DAY" at 1730 and dispatched CG-4300 at 1800. Due to heavy seas, this boat was unable to proceed and was recalled at 1900, arriving back at 2000.

b.   Charlevoix Lifeboat Station-Heard "MAY DAY" at 1731 and dispatched CG-36392 at 1815. This small boat was recalled at 1855 on the recommendation of Commanding Officer, CGC SUNDEW, due to heavy weather.

c.   Beaver Island Moorings -- CG-36505 held in readiness and was not dispatched to the scene due to the prevailing weather conditions and inexperience of the available personnel.

d.   USCGC SUNDEW (WAGL 4O4) Moored at Charlevoix Michigan, in a 12-hour stand-by status. The

SUNDEW was alerted by 1740 by the Group Commander, Charlevoix Group. The SUNDEW got underway at 1820 and arrived in the search area at 2240. The Commanding Officer, CGC SUNDEW, took over operational control of the search and coordinated the efforts of all units from this time on.

e. CG Air Station, Traverse City, Michigan -- This unit had one aircraft, UF 1273 returning from an air search in southern Lake Michigan and one aircraft UF 2135, in maintenance status. In addition, the station had two helicopters ready for flight; however, these were held in readiness, due to the prevailing weather conditions. UF 1273 was directed to proceed to the scene and arrived at 1915. The ceiling in the search area was 2,000 feet, and this aircraft was used throughout the night in the search and also to provide flare illumination for the surface vessels. A total of 88 flares were dropped during the night of 18-19 November. At daybreak, three H03S helicopters joined in the search, and the UF 2135 was dispatched to Beaver Island to provide gasoline for the helicopters.

f. CGC HOLLYHOCK (WAGL 220)--Moored at Sturgeon Bay, Wisconsin, in a 2-hour stand by status. The HOLLYHOCK was alerted by 1815 by operations Ninth Coast Guard District, Cleveland, Ohio, and was underway at 1830. The HOLLYHOCK arrived on the scene at 0230 and reported to the SUNDEW.

36. The SS ROBERT C. STANLEY, anchored at Garden Island, heard the "MAY DAY", got underway at 1824, and proceeded to the search area, arriving at midnight. This vessel was joined by other lake vessels and numerous military and civilian aircraft as the weather moderated and daylight on the 19th commenced. CG 40561, from Beaver Island Mooring, and CG-40499, from Charlevoix Lifeboat Station, joined the search on 19 November.

37. Four crewmen, including Fleming and Mays were able to board the life raft, which drifted rapidly away from the scene of the disaster. During the night, the other two were lost overboard as the raft flipped over several times in the heavy seas. The sea anchor also parted, leaving the raft completely at the mercy of the elements. At 0825 on 19 November, the SUNDEW sighted the raft with the two survivors, and Fleming and Mays were rescued at 0837 at a position 5 1/4 miles east northeast of Gull Island. An overturned lifeboat was sighted at 0930 at a position four miles east of Gull Island. This boat was not occupied and was later recovered off the southeast tip of High Island on the 21st. During the day 17 bodies were recovered by Coast Guard units in the area adjacent to the north of Gull Island. One body, that of Gary Strzelecki, one of the persons lost overboard from the raft during the night, was recovered by merchant vessel M/V TRANSONTARIO at 1314 at a position close to the west shore of High Island. Each body recovered had an approved cork lifejacket on, as did the two survivors.

38. A. The Following men survived: Total 2:

   (1) Elmer Fleming, North Bradley Highway
       Rogers City, Michigan

   (2) Frank Mays, 925 Linden Street
       Rogers City, Michigan

   B. The bodies of the following persons have been recovered; cause of death -- drowning: Total 18:

   (1) Carl R. Bartell, 357 North First Street
       Rogers City, Michigan

   (2) Alfred Boehmer, 455 South 4th Street,
       Rogers City, Michigan

(3) Richard J. Book, International Hotel,
Rogers City, Michigan

(4) Alva H. Budnick, Virgilene Trailer Court
Rogers City, Michigan

(5) William T. Elliot, Virgilene Trailer Court
Rogers City, Michigan

(6) Erhardt O. Felax, 685 South Lake Street
Rogers City, Michigan

(7) Cleland E. Gager
Onaway, Michigan

(8) Paul C. Heller, 1106 Riverview Street
Rogers City, Michigan

(9) Paul Horn, 448 North 4th Street
Rogers City, Michigan

(10) Raymond J. Kowalski, 1105 Dettloff Street
Rogers City, Michigan

(11) Joseph Krawczak, 645 South Second Street
Rogers City, Michigan

(12) Alfred Pilarski, 546 South Lake Street
Rogers City, Michigan

(13) Gary N. Price, P. O. Box 76
Onaway, Michigan

(14) Leo Promo, Jr., 419 St. Clair Street
Rogers City, Michigan

(15) Bernard Schefke, 506 South Lake Street
Rogers City, Michigan

(16) Gary Strzelecki, 234 West Michigan
     Rogers City, Michigan

(17) Edward N. Vallee, 206 Superior Street
     Rogers City, Michigan

(18) John Zoho, 853 Horton Avenue
     Clairton, Pennsylvania

c. The following men are missing Total 15:

   (1) Douglas Bellmore
       Onaway, Michigan

   (2) Roland O. Bryan
       Loudonville, New York

   (3) John F. Fogelsonger, Medora Street
       St. Ignace, Michigan

   (4) Raymond G. Buehler, 1500 Cordova Ave.
       Lakewood, Ohio

   (5) Clyde M. Enos, 410 Ball Street
       Cheboygan, Michigan

   (6) John L. Bauers, 316 Hilltop Lane
       Rogers City, Michigan

   (7) Keith Schuler, 314 North First Street
       Rogers City, Michigan

   (8) Duane Berg, 372 North Third Street
       Rogers City, Michigan

(9) Dennis Meredith, RFD
     Posen Michigan

(10) Floyd A. MacDougall, 144 South First St.
     Rogers City, Michigan

(11) Earl Tulgetske, Jr., 1012 Dottloff Street
     Rogers City, Michigan

(12) Paul Greengtski, RFD
     Posen, Michigan

(13) Melville Orr, 1113 Third Street
     Rogers City, Michigan

(14) Dennis Joppich, 457 South Second Street
     Rogers City, Michigan

(15) James L. Selke, 795 South First Street
     Rogers City, Michigan

39. All the persons reported to have been on watch in the engine room are among those still missing. Of the 18 bodies recovered, eight were from the forward end crew and ten were from the after end crew.

40. Radio station WAD, Fort Washington, assumed the radio control on channel 51 (2182 kc) in the SAR emergency and broadcast an order for radio silence at 1740. This initial order was repeated a number of times by WAD and other stations in the mideastern and eastern United States. The imposed radio silence was lifted an 1840 on 19 November and the active search was discontinued on 21 November 1958 by Office of the Commander, Ninth Coast Guard District, pending further developments. Serious interference

on channel 51 was reported. This interference was primarily from the unauthorized use of channel 51 by vessels on the Ohio and Mississippi Rivers and partly from the failure of Great Lakes area stations and vessels to maintain silence. The interference, however was not serious enough to interfere with the on scene communications among the vessels and planes actively engaged in the search.

41. Boulder Reef lighted bell buoy (LL 2163) was on station and showing its proper characteristics at 1410 on 19 November when checked by CGC SUNDEW.

42. In the vicinity of Boulder Reef, shoal water of 60 ft in depth or less extends over an area, which is approximately six miles long and three miles wide. The area circumscribed by this 60-foot depth curve runs mainly to the north northeast of Boulder Reef, which is marked on its southwest edge by Boulder Reef lighted buoy. The reef has a minimum depth of 15 feet adjacent to the buoy and shoal area of 30 feet of less extends to a distance of about 1.5 miles northward from the buoy.

43. Aircraft from Coast Guard Air Station; Traverse City spent a total of 122 hours searching the casualty area from 18 November to 9 December. During this time no evidence of the sunken hulks or large wreckage therefrom was sighted by the aircraft. Miscellaneous small pieces of wreckage were found, both by aircraft and searching parties, on the west shore of High and Beaver Islands. On 20 November, Coast Guard aircraft UF 2135 sighted on oil slick, resulting from oil bubbling to the surface from an underwater source. The source of this oil slick, which was feathering out downwind, was located 5 1/2 miles distant from Boulder Reef Buoy on

a bearing of 314° true. On 2 December 1958, the SUNDEW, sounding this area, noted on their depth recorder, type AN/UQW-IC, an irregularity in soundings which indicated a 25 foot pinnacle in 300 feet of water at the reported source of the oil slick. An immediate re-sounding this area failed to again show the pinnacle, and later attempts to relocate it have likewise proven unsuccessful. Attempts to locate the hulks by soundings were made by CGC MACKINAW (WAGB 83) and the SUNDEW during January and February; however unfavorable winter conditions curtailed these efforts. Further attempts will be make when weather conditions improve.

44. The Board takes judicial notice of the following facts:

a. Records indicate that November is a month of severe storms on the Great Lakes. The storm of 17—19 November 1958 has been described by various shipmasters as the most severe they have encountered. The publication "Shipwrecks of the Lakes", by Dana T. Bowen, reveals that between 1900 and 1950, over one-third of the vessels lost by foundering were lost during November, and over one half of all strandings occurred in November.

b. The trade followed by the self-unloading-type vessels is extremely hard on the vessels. The self-unloaders load and discharge many more cargoes per year than do the conventional bulk freighters, engaged in the iron ore trade. Likewise, these vessels frequent out of the way places in shallow water and often ground and rub bottom while approaching docks. In addition, because of the short hauls between loading and unloading parts, the self-unloaders spend considerably more time at near maximum speed in the shallow rivers then do conventional lake vessels.

c. The past inspection books, dry-dock examination

books, and other official records of the Coast Guard were examined by the board, and they revealed nothing of note concerning the CARL D. BRADLEY, except as mentioned elsewhere in the record concerning the last dry-docking in 1957 at Chicago, Illinois.

d. The official survey records of Lloyd's Register of Shipping were examined by the Board, and these records revealed nothing of note concerning the CARL D. BRADLEY. Extracts from the survey, in conjunction with the dry-docking in 1957 at Chicago, Illinois, are included with the record.

e. Section 726 of Department of the Navy Publication NWP-37, Search and Rescue, indicates that the wind current would be up to 30° to the right of the wind direction in direction of 045° true to 075° true.

OPINIONS

1. That the CARL D. BRADLEY did not strike Boulder Reef, but that she broke in half in deep water in a position about five miles to the northwestward of Boulder Reef.

2. That the vessel could not have proceeded for more than one mile between the time of the initial thud and the time she broke in half, and the CARL D. BRADLEY continued on course during this period.

3. That had the vessel struck Boulder Reef, both parts of the hulk, by reason of their dimension, would be visible in the water of less than 60- foot depth, which extends for a distance of about three miles northeast of the reef along the track the CARL D. BRADLEY would have made.

4. And further, that having in mind the manner in which the vessel broke and the way the stern section plunged to the bottom, the CARL D. BRADLEY sank in water considerably deeper than 60 feet.

5. Supporting the opinion that the CARL D. BRADLEY did not strike Boulder Reef and the facts established relative to the navigation of both the CARL D. BRADLEY and the M/V CHRISTIAN SARTORI.

6. That the cause of the casualty was due to the excessive hogging stresses imposed upon the vessel by reason of her placement in a ballasted condition upon the waves encountered at the particular instant of breaking. There were no facts disclosed by the testimony, or through examination of the files on the CARL D. BRADLEY maintained by the U.S. Coast Guard, or Lloyd's Registry of Shipping, which would lead to an opinion that there existed any defects in the area where the break occurred. However, it is felt that the appearance of hairline fractures in the vessel's bottom plating as found in drydock, may be of significance in a technical study of this casualty by the Ships' Structure Committee, or other technical body, although the Board could fine no indication of a relationship between this casualty and those earlier-noted hairline fractures.

7. That the eruption of steam, flames, and smoke noticed by the survivors and the CHRISTIAN SARTORI, occurred after the vessel parted, and was caused by water rushing into the combustion chambers of the boilers as the stern section plunged. The fact that all bodies from the after end that were recovered were victims of drowning, with no indication of burns or violence, supports the conclusion that the reported explosion was actually the eruption of steam and combustible material from the boiler out through the stack.

206

8. That the vessel was seaworthy at the time of completion of her annual inspection at Calcite, Michigan on 17 April 1958, and that there is no reason to conclude from the testimony or from reasonable interpretation of other known facts that she was not in such condition upon departure from Gary, Indiana, on 17 November 1958.

9. That the vessel was properly manned and equipped in accordance with existing regulations and properly secured for sea upon departure from Gary, Indiana.

10. That the temporary repairs to the cargo hold, made in the winter 1957-58 did not contribute to this casualty.

11. That the two unreported damages known to have been incurred during the 1958 season at Cedarville, Michigan, were minor in nature and of such location on the hull as to not have contributed to this casualty.

12. That the watertight door in bulkhead 173 at the forward end of the machinery spaces was not completely dogged at the time of the casualty, and that the watertight integrity of the vessel was thereby impaired, It appears likely that the door became undogged by some reason unknown and then swung open, allowing the free entry of the water from the tunnel to the engine spaces. It is felt, had the door been completely dogged and thus maintained bulkhead 173 watertight, additional buoyancy would have been provided, and the speed with which the stern section sank would have been materially reduced.

13. That the drowning of some of those crewmen whose bodies were recovered were caused by inhalation of the heavy spray. Because of the low water and air temperatures, and extremely rough seas, no type of lifejacket could have enabled

207

any person to survive the 16-hour ordeal in the water. Further, that the type of lifejacket worn by the victims caused fatigue by reason of the need to exert constant arm pressure on the jacket to keep it down on the body while in the water. It is the opinion of the Board that the cork life preservers are not a satisfactory type for sustained support in the water because of the way they fit.

14. That the drift and set of the life raft, lifeboat, and bodies carried them north of Gull Island and to the eastward. This drift and set is in fair agreement with what might be expected from the information contained in Section 725 of NWP 37, Search and Rescue Manual, although it is realized that the application of the theories developed in this manual to the relatively shallow waters of the area in question might not be unqualifiedly accepted.

15. That efforts made by the crew in attempting to lower the starboard lifeboat were thwarted by the short time the stern section remained on an even keel. With the prevailing weather conditions and the quick settling of the after section, it is considered extremely doubtful that a launching of a lifeboat in the variety of the vessel's counter by use of falls fitted with common hooks could have been successfully accomplished.

16. That the search and rescue operations in this casualty were thorough and well directed. All Coast Guard units responded to the maximum of their ability under the existing weather conditions, and the major floating units were underway well within the period allowed by their standby status. The appreciation of the survivors and the representatives of the owners of the CARL D. BRADLEY for the efforts of the CGC SUNDEW is worthy of note. The decision of the responsible personnel attached to the Coast Guard Air Station to hold the

available helicopters for actual rescue work in view of the weather condition was based on sound judgement.

17. That participation of the M/V CHRISTIAN SARTORI in the search was in keeping with finest traditions of the sea. This vessel was immediately headed toward the scene of the casualty, and made every effort to assist under extremely adverse weather conditions. The fact that the searching of the SARTORI proved unsuccessful does not detract from the valiant efforts of the Master and crew to aid the crew of CARL D. BRADLEY. The voluntary participation by other merchant vessels, as well as private, commercial, and military aircraft, and by the individual citizens of the various islands was also commendable.

18. That communication pursuant to this SAR emergency was adequate. All situations in the area maintained radio silence when so directed, and the interference on channel 51 that did occur did not impede communications on the scene.

19. That had the life raft been equipped with rocket or parachute-type distress signals, the survivors might have been located during the night.

20. That it is the stated policy of the owners of the CARL D. BRADLEY to give the masters complete responsibility for the safety of their vessels and, therefore, complete freedom to anchor or postpone departure, if unfavorable weather or other reasons dictate such action to be in the interests of safety. In view of this, it is the opinion of the Board that the master of the CARL D. BRADLEY, in making the decision to and in proceeding across northern Lake Michigan from Cana Island toward Lansing Shoal, exercised poor judgment. This decision was probably induced by a zealous desire to hold as

209

closely to schedule as possible, and because of this, he gave less attention to the dangers of the existing weather than what might be expected of a prudent mariner.

21. That no aids to navigation or uncharted or incorrectly charted area or objects were involved in the casualty.

22. That no personnel of the Coast Guard or any other governmental agency contributed to the casualty.

23. That there is no evidence that any licensed or certificated personnel of the CARL D. BRADLEY committed any acts of incompetence, inattention to duty, negligence or willful violation of any law or regulation.

RECOMMENDATIONS

1. That all jacket-type life preservers be provided with a crotch strap to hold the jacket down on the body and with a collar to support the head out of water. In this respect, the specifications for life preservers under 46 CFR 180.002.005 (Subchapter Q, Specifications) will require modification.

2. That a second additional life raft or other approved buoyant apparatus be mandatory for all Great Lakes cargo vessels of 300 gross tons and that 46 CFR 94.10-40(a) and 16 CFR 94.15.10(c)(3) (Subchapter I, Cargo and Miscellaneous Vessels) be modified to require two life rafts and to specify that one of these rafts shall be in the forward part of the vessel and one in the after part of the vessel.

3. That each lifeboat on all Great Lake cargo vessels of over 3000 gross tons be fitted with mechanical disengaging apparatus. To effect this recommendation the provision of 46 CFR 94.10.5(3) (4)(i) should be modified to include

Great Lakes vessels and to require that all existing common hook installations be replaced with mechanical disengaging apparatus at the earliest possible date. Further, that the provisions of this recommendations to be extended to include all Great Lakes tank and passenger vessels of over 3000 gross tons, and that the applicable sections of 46 CFR, Part 33 (Subchapter D, Tank Vessel), and 46 CFR, Part 75 (Subchapter 11, Passenger Vessels), be so modified.

4. That each lifeboat and life raft on all Great Lakes cargo vessels be equipped with two painters as required for ocean and coastwise vessels, and that 46 CFR 94.20.10 (a) and 46 CFR 94.20.15 (a) be modified accordingly. Further, that the provisions of this recommendation be extended to include all Great Lakes tank and passenger vessels, and that the applicable sections of 46 CFR, Part 33 (Subchapter D Tank Vessels) and 46 CFR, Part 75 (Subchapter H Passenger Vessels), be so modified.

5. That each lifeboat and life raft on all Great Lakes cargo vessels be provided with a unit of at least six red parachute type flare distress signals and the means to project them. This recommendation will require modification of 46 CFR 94.20.10 (a) 46 CFR 94.20.20 (a) 46 CFR 94.20.15 (hh), and 46 CFR 94.20.25 (m). Further, that the provisions of this recommendation be extended to include all Great Lakes tank and passenger vessels, and that applicable section of 46 CFR, Part 33 (Subchapter D, Tank Vessels), and 46 CFR, Part 75 (Subchapter H, Passenger Vessels), be so modified.

6. Inasmuch as the exact location of the hull of the CARL D. BRADLEY is unknown at this time and the possibility exists that reasonable efforts to locate the hull during this coming shipping season will be successful, which may or may not alter the findings of fact, opinions, or recommendations of

this board, it is recommend that the board remain in adjourned status so that it may be reconvened should circumstances demand.

Joseph Kerrins - Rear Admiral, U.S. Coast Guard
    Chairman
Charles E. Leising - Commander, U.S. Coast Guard
    Member
Joseph Change - Commander, U.S. Coast Guard
    Member
Garth H. Read - Lieutenant Commander, U.S. Coast Guard
    Member and Recorder

Appendix G.

Out of the Blue Productions

Jim and Pat Stayer along with their friend Tim Juhl formed Out of the Blue Productions in the early 1990's with the goal of locating and documenting Great Lakes shipwrecks so that others could enjoy taking a "step back in time." Accomplished SCUBA Divers, the trio has been very successful in that endeavor and have shared many adventures exploring the depths of both the Great Lakes and the oceans of the world. Their work has been shown to audiences in many major cities and has appeared on TV stations from all the major networks. In addition to producing an ever-increasing number of video and DVD programs, the trio has written three books. These are:

Shipwrecks of Sanilac – A diver's and historian's look at the shipwrecks of the *Sanilac Shores Underwater Preserve* in lower Lake Huron.

Sole Survivor – Coauthored with survivor Dennis Hale, tells the story of the 1966 sinking of the *SS Daniel J. Morrell*. In the book, Hale recounts the sinking and his incredible 38 hour ordeal on a tiny raft on storm-lashed Lake Huron.

If We Make It 'til Daylight – Coauthored with survivor Frank Mays, tells the story of the 1958 sinking of the *SS Carl D. Bradley*. In the book, Frank's story is joined by that of others who played an important role in the search and rescue. The result of this collaboration is one of the most incredible shipwreck tales to come from the Great Lakes in the past century.

In addition to producing videos and books, beginning in 1996, <u>Out of the Blue Productions</u> hosted a number of programs in Port Huron, Michigan, called *Shipwrecks Remembered*. Held annually in November, each show featured programs about ships that have been lost in the Great Lakes and elsewhere. Since its inception, numerous survivors and other notables appeared on the program, which was considered to be one of the best of its kind in the Great Lakes region. DVDs of these programs are available.

For more information or to order books or DVDs, visit: www.outoftheblueproductions.net

Appendix H.
About the Authors
Updated 2018
Frank Mays - This is his story.
We're happy to report Frank is still living life to the fullest, traveling around the world touring different countries.

Frank Mays visiting the *Cedarville* and *Bradley*
memorial In Rogers City
Photo Credit--Tim Juhl

Jim Stayer – Jim is retired from the Port Huron School District, where he taught Science, Math, and Video Production to high school students. As a U.S. Coast Guard licensed captain, Jim, along with his wife Pat ran a charter boat for over 20 years. The couple is well known

Photo Credit--Jim and Pat Stayer

for their shipwreck discoveries and explorations in the

Photo Credit--Pat Stayer

Great Lakes. A skilled underwater videographer, Jim has earned a reputation among divers and historians alike for his role in helping to preserve and document Great Lakes shipwreck history.

Pat Stayer – Pat is retired from Carsonville-Port Sanilac Schools where she taught third grade for much of her career. A gifted underwater photographer and videographer herself, Pat works tirelessly on all the group's projects and is the glue that holds everything together.

Photo Credit--Jim Stayer

215

Her skill and artistry is responsible for the outstanding graphics and effects that appear in the group's books and videos. In 2005, Pat was inducted to the Women Divers Hall of Fame for her diving-related accomplishments.

Since retiring, Jim and Pat have branched out to exploring the world. The pair are considered to be among the best marine animal behavior videographers and are much in demand for their programs on new and unique saltwater dive destinations.

Tim Juhl –Tim is retired from Carsonville-Port Sanilac Schools, where he taught Video Production and Science. A diver since 1965, Tim brought a wealth of experience in video production to the group. His writing skills and mellow narrator's voice appear in many of the group's projects. Tim enjoys Great Lake's maritime history and considers the opportunity to work with Frank Mays and Dennis Hale on their biographies to be among

Photo Credit--Cris Kohl

the great privileges of his life. Discovering and exploring long lost shipwrecks along with his good friends is a close second.

Photo Credit--Tim Juhl

A PADI Master Diver as well as a commercial pilot and flight instructor, Tim has enjoyed many exciting hours both beneath the water's surface and high above it.